MY SOFTBALL SCHOLARSHIP

MY SOFTBALL SCHOLARSHIP

Living the Dream of Earning a College Softball Scholarship

Jeff Poulton . Emily Poulton

www.mysoftballscholarship.com

Outskirts Press, Inc.
Denver, Colorado

Outskirts Press, Inc.
http://www.outskirtspress.com

ISBN: 978-1-4327-3707-8

Outskirts Press and the "OP" logo are trademarks belonging to Outskirts Press, Inc.

PRINTED IN THE UNITED STATES OF AMERICA

About the Authors:

Dad: $

After receiving a Bachelor of Science degree in Education from the University of Massachusetts where he met his wife Tracy; Jeff began his 23-year career with one of the largest automobile and mortgage financing companies in the US. He has co-authored several training workbooks throughout his tenure there. Jeff has also traveled extensively throughout the country visiting almost every state, conducting training workshops. He currently works in Southern California where he resides with his wife Tracy and three daughters; Rachel, Emily, and Justine.

Emily:

A graduate of Great Oak High School in Temecula, CA, Emily is attending a NCAA Division II College on the east coast where she is playing for their softball team on scholarship. Emily has played softball since she was able to throw a ball when she started in Little League T-ball. After winning the title of California State Champion, her 12-U All-Star Little League team advanced to the Regional play-offs where they came within one game of entering the Little League World Series. Her 14-U ASA travel ball team ended their season in 7th place in the ASA National Tournament. Emily's most recent softball "wow" moment was during the summer between her Junior and Senior year in high school when she was able to play with an ASA Women's Open Team. The Australian National Team stopped in California on their way home from a loss to Team

USA where Emily got in a couple of innings "behind the dish" against Australia. It was quite a thrill for her to be the youngest person involved in the event. Emily's college career is just beginning as of the publishing date so that chapter has yet to be written.

Emily also has a passion for music. As an accomplished percussionist, Emily has played with her high school marching band, winter drum line, church, and several live community theater productions.

It is Emily's life long love of softball, her commitment and hard work, culminating in a college scholarship that inspired this book.

Dedication:

To all the young ladies who have a dream to attend college on a softball scholarship…

Acknowledgements:

Although the cover of <u>My Softball Scholarship</u> bears my name as the primary author, no book is written without the help of many hands and minds. I acknowledge them here for their care in tutoring a novice writer.

Thank you Nels Jenson for being the first to read the manuscript and for the kind words of encouragement. My first draft was in rough shape. You not only read it three times, but typed your notes to me too! The time you took for this thankless task was more than I could have ever expected.

Thank you Wanda Bledsoe. You helped me to "get my mind around the big picture." You took a small mustard seed and turned it into a mighty tree. All this in the time it took to eat a cup of soup and a salad.

Hugs, kisses, and a "Thank You" to my beautiful wife Tracy and daughters Rachel and Justine for putting up with my many hours of pontificating about writing and publishing this book. You read it in its infancy and helped tremendously with the editing process. I love you with all my heart.

A special loving "Thank You" to my daughter Emily for your bravery, for sharing your story so others might benefit, and for co-authoring this text with me. God has blessed you with a heart of gold. You never cease to amaze me with your acts of grace and kindness toward others. I love you with all my heart as well...

Table Of Contents:

Introduction i

Chapter I
Living the Dream! 1
Who Is This Workbook For? 6
Getting Started 8
When Do I Start? How Do I Start? 12
Goal Setting 12
    Writing the Goal 13
        S.M.A.R.T. Goals 13
    Using the Written Goal to Influence Every Decision You Make........15
Grades 16
How to Use this Book..17
    What is Next in Chapter II? 17
    What is Next in Chapter III? 17
    Clarification of Appendix A 18
    Additional Resources 18

Chapter II
Schedule During Grades 9 – 12 21
Freshman Year (9th Grade) 22
Sophomore Year (10th Grade) 23

Junior Year (11th Grade) 23
Senior Year (12th Grade) 24

Chapter III
Steps to Success 27
Step 1 -Visit the College Board, NCAA, NAIA, and NJCAA Web Sites 27
Step 2 -Creating a College List 33
Step 3 -Skills Video 36
Step 4 -Making Contact 39
    Show Case Events 43
    Player Profile Sample 45
    College Clinics 47
Step 5 -Respond to Questionnaires and Other Inquiries 48
    Things Are Heating Up Now 52
Step 6 -Visiting Colleges 55
    Official Visit 55
    Unofficial Visit 55
Step 7 -The Application 64
    Early Decision 65
    Early Action 65
    Single Choice Early Action 65
    Regular Acceptance Period 65
Step 8 -The Offer - National Letter of Intent (NLI) 66
    Financial Aid Information 67
Step 9 -What Happens After I Sign? 69

Chapter IV
Other Stuff Just for Grins and Giggles 73
Picking a Club/Travel Team 73
Play Time with your Club/Travel Team 73
Team Coach and Public Relations (PR) Coach 74
Professional Athlete vs. Professional Student 74
Peer Reaction 75
High School and Club/Travel Coaches as a Resource 75

Emily's Closing Comments 76

www.mysoftballscholarship.com 78

Appendix A – College List 79

Reach Schools 79

Attainable Schools 88

Safety Schools 118

Other/Maybe 121

Coach Contacted Me But Not On My List 124

Introduction

Emily:

The memory is burned into my brain like it just happened yesterday. I had played plenty of softball so standing on third base and running home when the ball was hit was as second nature to me as breathing and blinking my eyes. We were practicing under the lights again. It was cold out that night but not too cold to play. The park where we practiced was well lit thanks to the huge lights in the park. But beyond the field, it was black. I mean really black. You couldn't see two feet in front of your face out there past the lights. Thank God I wasn't playing outfield tonight. It was creepy out there.

Running the bases was something I liked to do. It kept me warm and I could run fast. The ball was hit high into the air as I immediately jumped off the bag and ran to home plate as fast as I could. Instead of hearing cheering voices and getting high fives, it was quiet. I looked around after tagging home base to see my Coach shaking his head at me (again). The left fielder was holding the softball in her glove as she stood right where the light met the wall of black. She casually threw it to third base where the girl at third easily touched the bag for the third out. I forgot to tag up. It was only practice so no big deal right? Besides, practice was almost over anyway.

When the Coach motioned for me to come back to third, I sprinted back to the bag. I knew the punishment for not hustling at practice. Thankfully, I never had to run for lack of hustle but I ran for plenty of other reasons. He yelled to the team to start running. "Run to where the black starts and then keep going! Poulton, you stay here at third base." He made them run for quite a while that night. I felt terrible. As my friends were running themselves silly for my error, I just stood at third base watching them. Coach slowly walked up to me and leaned in really close so no one else could hear him except for me. "Poulton, you can't throw, you can't hit, you can't field, you can't run, you can't do anything right. You can't play softball. You're pretty and smart all right, but I have no idea why you're on this field. Softball is not your sport. You should give up." Then he just walked away. My friends slowly came staggering in after running. They didn't hold it against me though. They knew it easily could have been any one of them standing on third base.

That memory has always stayed with me. I knew from that point on that I was going to keep playing and not give up. That moment motivated me to keep trying and not let someone like that tell me what I could or couldn't do. I knew deep down that I was capable of succeeding, even if he didn't believe in me. I was 14 years old when that happened but I was never going to let anyone kill my dream! If it was ever going to die, that was a decision that I reserved solely for myself.

Emily: ✒ (cont.)

Hi there! My name is Emily and this is my story. Thank you for checking out the book that my dad and I wrote. I know that first story is "heavy", but it really happened, just like all the other stories that you'll read going forward. We put this book together so you can see how I traveled through the journey of earning a college scholarship by playing softball. But before you continue reading, I just wanted to give you a quick heads up on how we laid out the book. When you see this font and this symbol: **Emily:** ✒ , you'll know that it's me, Emily writing. When you see this font (that's the serious one ha ha) and this symbol: **Dad:** $, you'll know it's my dad. His name is Jeff. My dad is going to start off the book with a quick note to you and your parents but you will see me back again really soon. Ok, now that we have that cleared up, enjoy the rest of the book. I really hope it helps you to reach your goal of living the dream of earning a college softball scholarship!

1
Living The Dream!

Dad: $

All of us softball parents have done it. Our daughters were playing softball at yet another practice, a friendly, Little League, or perhaps a Travel Softball Tournament in some far off land when the thought came up that always comes up after we sat watching our girls. We don't exactly come right out and say it outright. Instead, when talking to the other parents, we dance around it like two ballerinas in a skillfully choreographed number on a Broadway show. But at the end of the conversation, the same question is running through almost every parent's mind. Is she good enough to make it to college on a softball scholarship? I hope so… I really hope so…

You see, we are all very proud of our daughters. But we don't want to come off <u>too</u> proud. That's just not cool. So we dance. Anyone who has been blessed with a daughter who has realized any level of success in a competitive softball program knows exactly what I'm talking about.

I consider Emily to be a very lucky young lady. She loves to play softball and we live in Southern California. The two go together like peanut butter and jelly. California is what I would call a "hot bed" for the sport due to its warm climate lending itself to a year round playing environment. As a result, the level of play is extremely high and competitive. As with most sports, the more you play, the better you get. You can't spit in Southern California without hitting a softball tournament somewhere in your immediate area. Nice analogy, huh? You get the point. SoCal also draws a group of very talented coaches as well. As you read in Emily's story, they can be tough. But the stakes are high so "tough" is what you sometimes get, depending on the level of the team your daughter plays on. But when you put a talented coach together with a talented athlete, you'll definitely see some great things happen. The end result is simple. As I say to Emily all the time, "You are living the dream!" The sacrifices, the work, the focus, and of course the time commitment... It all paid off one October morning at a coffee shop over some bagels at breakfast. But we will get to that later…

Before we get into the process that helped Emily earn a college scholarship, let's hear from Emily again so she can tell us the events that led to her getting really excited about softball.

Emily:

I wanted to tell you how it all started for me. I was playing Little League in the local 12U Division where I live. My team had an ok year. My dad was the coach and we ran in the middle of the pack, not the champions, but not the bottom of the barrel either. Ok, I'll come clean; sometimes we were the bottom of the barrel. But we had our moments of greatness too. Anyway, after the regular season was over, I was lucky enough to make the All Star team. I knew all the other girls on the team and they were good softball players. I had many memories of getting my butt kicked when playing against them, but I never played <u>with</u> them. This was a new experience for sure. I had also never made an All Star team before so I wasn't sure what it was all about. My coach let me know right away. I went from practicing a couple of times a week to practicing every single day. In case you've never been to Southern California in the summer time, we live in a desert so it's hot and dry. Those practices were tough but they paid off. None of the other coaches or players from our league had any real faith that we would win any games. As players, we didn't know any better so we just went out and played for the love of the game. It was awesome! We won the first tournament so we were District Champions. Then we went on to win the Section Tournament and Southern California Division. Now people were starting to notice. Everyone back home was talking about us. A local reporter even wrote an article about us and put our picture in the newspaper.

Traveling to Portland, Oregon to represent Southern California in the Regional Tournament was the pinnacle of the summer. The Little League World Series was now just one step away. I could hardly believe it. We even drove over to the field where they play the World Series games to see what it was like in case we made it there. I got to walk on the grass, kick some dirt in the infield, and sit in the dugout. We ended up beating Northern California in that tournament so we were the California State Champs but we fell short of getting into the World Series. We found out after we got home that the team that beat us ended up getting disqualified for having an ineligible player. It's ironic that we would have gotten into the World Series after all but it was too late. We had already traveled home. The tournaments took almost all summer long so most of the parents had used up all their money and vacation time from work so we couldn't really go back to Oregon after coming home. I can tell you that this summer was the spark that got me going. I got a taste of competitive softball and I wanted more!

Emily in her 12u - All Star Uniform

Dad: $

Emily jumped right into "fall ball" after returning home from Portland. It's a recreational softball league scheduled in the fall in California for girls who want to keep their skills sharp. Following fall ball, she was ready for a competitive travel softball team. She was on her way… Within a short two year time frame after that Little League All-Star team, Emily decided that she would like to play softball in college. She was now playing for a travel team that was ranked among the leaders in the country so things were getting more serious on the softball field. She was now at the point in her softball career where she was playing or practicing almost every day of the week. If she was lucky, she had one day of rest every week. It was very intense. I kept asking her if this is what she wanted and if this was fun for her. Her answer was always the same. "Yes, I'm having fun." She couldn't get enough. She demonstrated a very high level of commitment so once she verbalized her goal of wanting to play softball in college at the young age of 14 years old, like most parents, I set out to support her in whatever fashion I could. Let the games begin… I had no idea what I had agreed to.

When I first started attending Emily's weekend softball events, I have to admit that I felt like a fish out of water. There was a certain language and choreography to this "dance". I quickly found that I had two left feet. Having a sales background, my professional training and instinct told me to do what I do best; ask questions and that's exactly what I did.

It is easy to understand that most parents are very eager to talk about their child. I was able to get most of my questions answered from other parents and coaches. I learned that the really gifted athletes with good grades had little to worry about. Some of those girls had a gift and they knew how to use it. I call them "born athletes" but in retrospect, I don't think that's a fair label. Even for the most gifted athletes, there are hours and hours of work that occurs behind the scenes. What we see during game time is usually the result of many hours of practice off the field. Never-the-less, those girls who are talented enough to get into the coveted NCAA Division I (DI) program of their choice on a full scholarship, are the exception to the rule. As your daughter matures from T-ball to coach pitch to player pitch, you start to get a feel for the standouts. As your daughter works up through the ranks, you can see how your daughter's abilities compare with the rest of the girls on the field.

With that in mind, I saw plenty of really good athletes that, for one reason or another, just were not going to be a good fit for a Division I athletic program. It was a case of what I call the "enoughs". Some were not big enough, tall enough, committed enough, putting enough "A's" on their report card, etc. Some did not want it enough, at least not at that level. They may want to spend time playing softball but they may also want to do other things too. There are millions of reasons why a DI school isn't a good fit but it is important for your daughter to figure that out for herself if she can. This process will help her do just that! So what happens to the rest of the girls? What do they do? What happens if they don't get into a D1 program on a full scholarship?

The concept for this book was born out of one unanswered question that arose during numerous conversations I personally had with many of the parents throughout the years at countless softball tournaments I attended. That question was this:

What is the process for high school student athletes who are looking to successfully transition from high school to college while earning a scholarship to play collegiate softball?

I was shocked to learn how few of the parents I spoke to actually had any idea of what to do. They didn't know how to get started or what to do next if they had started. I saw many talented softball players never realize their dream of playing at the college level because a lack of the knowledge of the process. The fallout over the years was painful to witness as some of these girls were really good softball players and great kids too. As a result, Emily and I decided to document Emily's story for others that might benefit from both of our perspectives in the process of earning a softball scholarship.

As you read this book, you will quickly find that it is unique in a few ways. First of all, you will benefit from it as a workbook. It is meant to be used over and over again. Feel free to fold over the corners of the pages that are important to you, write all over it, and refer back to it often. The second unique feature is that you are going to get the information from two different views. You will hear information from Emily (the softball player) and me, Jeff (Emily's father). As a result, both parents and players will want to use this tool to work through the process.

Both <u>Parents</u> and <u>Players</u> will want to use this tool to work through the process!

This book is also different from others in that you most likely won't read it cover-to-cover. You will jump around a little depending on where you are in the process of earning your softball college scholarship and what grade you attend at your high school. This is normal because it is a workbook. Key word here is "work". If you are a softball player, that term is not new to you…

Who Is This Workbook For?

Dad: $

This workbook is meant to be used as a tool for parents and high school student athletes while earning a scholarship to play collegiate softball. I will refer to student athletes as an "**SA**" throughout this book. Although some who will use this manual are high level sport prodigies or "hot shots" who are highly sought after by many Division I college programs, this workbook is geared more towards the athlete who has a mid-to-high level of academic standing and is considered an average-to-above average athlete. This target audience is sometimes considered for Division I programs, but more likely will focus more effort on NCAA Division II and III (DII and DIII), NAIA and Junior College programs. It is also a plan that will require a commitment from the SA in terms of time and effort. It's based on one simple belief:

> **There is a college softball scholarship for every SA**
> **who is willing to put in the effort to find it!**

Before I go any further, here are some assumptions that I am making about your SA.

- As an SA, you are just that, a student and an athlete in high school, grade 12 or below.
- The SA is actively involved in softball at a non-professional level, not just playing once in a while at a recreational level. The SA must be involved with softball almost year round to some extent. If they are not actively playing now, they are

preparing physically and mentally for the next season or off-season. This can involve working out, resting an injury, or focusing on school work.

- The SA participates in softball in high school and/or outside of high school with a club or private team. This is a rule of thumb but not always the case due to geographic restrictions and personal circumstances. Everyone's situation is different. Just be sure you actively play the sport!
- The SA participates in the activity of her own free will. She participates because she has a deep desire to play at a competitive level and to excel at her sport.
- The SA has access to a computer and a basic understanding of the internet.
- The SA has an adult (parent, coach, teacher, counselor, or relative) available to them to answer basic questions, provide guidance, and to assist with the process and moral support.
- The SA values the importance of an education.
- The SA and adult guide are willing and able to do most of the recruiting work in this workbook themselves.

With that said, this book will help address the following comments and questions that I've heard from many SA's and their parents:

- "I can do this! I'm a good player! I'm willing to do the work. I just need to know how."
- "How do I get started?"
- "I'm not quite sure of the process."
- "Is there somewhere I can go to get some answers? I just have a quick question that will only take a second to answer and then I'll be off and running."
- "I just need a little help from someone who's been there, done that!"
- "OK, so I'm not a Division I player, but are there other options out there for me to play my sport in college?"
- "How do I get a college recruiter to look at me at the showcase events?"
- "Are there college softball programs where I can play but not have to practice for five hours every single day?"
- "During and after I read this book, is there somewhere I can go to get additional support?"

Do these questions sound familiar? Right, I thought so… If you've heard yourself saying any of these comments before, keep reading. You're already headed in the right direction.

Parents, you may be asking:

How do I turn this…   into this?

Getting Started:

Dad: $

The main point here is that getting into college and being able to play your sport is not a one-time event that happens when you sign the acceptance letter. It is a process that usually takes several years to complete.

> **"It's not a one-time event; it's a process that takes several years to complete."**

If that statement concerns you, then you need to re-evaluate your desire to go through this process. You will experience moments of extreme happiness along with times of despair and deep concern. Emily and I had many arguments throughout her softball experience; everything from play time, to finances, to work habits, to grades, to passion, etc. SA's will argue with their parents. Parents will sometimes challenge the SA to work harder. Anyone involved in sports at a competitive level knows all too well about this part of the game. Just know that it will carry over into this process as well. My advice is to keep it in check. One win or loss on the field usually does not determine an athlete's legacy. Nor will it in the recruiting game.

Another thing to consider as you go through this journey is to keep your options open. You will see this statement repeated throughout the book.

"The larger the net you cast, the more fish you will catch!"

As I mentioned in the beginning of this book, California is a "hot bed" for softball. Great opportunity is the upside. However, great competition in terms of college recruiting can be the downside to that equation. So what I mean by "casting a large net" is for you to consider many colleges throughout the country. The more colleges you consider, the better your chances are of getting into one and getting a softball scholarship. This may seem obvious but it's a conscious decision you'll have to make at some point in this process. I'm not saying that you should avoid trying to attend college close to home. Just know that there are only so many colleges around your house. Those colleges have only so many softball positions to fill and only so many scholarships to offer.

Let's look at some numbers. Assume a college team carries about fifteen players. If there are 25 colleges within driving distance of your house, perhaps five of them or 20% will be a good fit for you in terms of academics and type of softball program. Out of those five, maybe two or three will need someone to fill the position that you play in the year that you're being recruited. There might be 50 or more girls trying to get that one position. The odds are stacked against you. Now let's say that you are willing to go anywhere in the US. There are thousands of colleges available to you with hundreds that will be a good fit in terms of academics and softball program. There will be many coaches looking to fill many positions. So instead of being one of 50 or more girls trying to get two or three positions, you'll be competing to get thousands of positions available. The chances of you being a good fit for the college and the college being a good fit for you are greatly increased with larger numbers!

Emily:

I think I was lucky in this area. But I improved my luck with a "large net" as my dad says. I always knew that I wanted to go to a college somewhere on the east coast and I knew fairly early that I didn't want to pursue softball at a DI college. But I would add that in addition to playing the numbers game, there are other factors that go into the type of college you attend. It's a very personal choice and can take a long time to figure out. Here are the factors that went into my decision to choose to play at a DII college softball program.

The first and most important reason was that I wanted a large emphasis on academics. I spend almost as many hours studying as I do playing softball. I'm one of those kids who go to the library every night after softball practice to study. Grades are very important to me and my family. So that part of my game always came first for me. I know it sounds funny to say grades are a part of my game, but they really are. I think grades are actually the most important part. I learned through some of my friends that without good grades, many of the colleges that they wanted to attend had closed their doors to them. It's one of the first things that college coaches look at; especially if you're looking at DII, DIII, NAIA, or a Junior College.

The second reason I decided to play at a DII school has a story to it so here it is. When I was 14 years old playing travel ball, I was on one of those teams that won almost all the time. We expected to win and we did win. We finished in 7th place that year at ASA Nationals. Those girls were not only great friends, but they were some of the most talented softball players I had ever seen. Almost all the girls on that team expected to go to a DI college. It was such an intense program; so intense that a few of the girls burned out and don't even play anymore. But the fact of the matter is that most of the girls who are still playing from that team are going to DI colleges on full scholarships. I wasn't a starter on that team. I was a utility player and I played off the bench. It was tough to do but I accepted my role and tried to make the best out of every opportunity that was presented to me.

When we attended tournaments, there were DI scouts at every game. But I knew they weren't watching me. I came to the conclusion that while I felt that I may have been good enough to play DI softball, I most likely didn't have a very good chance. I now know that accepting this fact when I was 14 helped my search as I got into high school because I wasn't wasting my time looking at college softball programs that weren't a good fit for me. You have to be realistic about your abilities on and off the field.

The third factor was all about time commitment. I work really hard on my softball game but after taking an honest look at myself, I didn't feel that a DI program would be a good fit for me in terms of time commitment. From what I learned from speaking with other college athletes that I knew, the DI players spent a lot more time on softball than the DII players did. The DII players spent more time on softball than the DIII players did. And so on... While I love softball, I wanted to be able to experience other things in college that are outside of softball; things like student groups, volunteer activities, and of course, studying.

With all that said, I still wanted a very competitive college softball experience too since I had played on some very high level teams. Once you get a taste for that level of success, you want to have the chance to live it again as I'm sure many of you would agree. To me, DII seemed to fit all of those requirements as a general rule of thumb; a high focus on academics and a focus on a high level of competitive softball within a reasonable amount of time spent during my daily routine.

For me the decision to look across the country allowed me to get away from competing with all the California girls for all the California colleges. Once I really started to focus on specific colleges in my junior year in high school, I started to realize that there is definitely more opportunity across the country. There are so many schools that you don't even realize are out there. I knew a lot of girls that said that if you don't go to a big DI college, you can't go anywhere. But there are many other non-DI schools that have money for you and are looking for talent. You never know until you look for them. You just have to broaden your approach when looking.

I also learned that there are a lot of people who like to go to college close to their home. This is true for any state in the US. So I knew that if I was OK to attend college somewhere else, away from home, I would open up the number of colleges available to me by hundreds of schools and thousands of positions or "slots" on those teams. I think this is one of the biggest reasons that I was able to find a college that was a good fit for me. I considered colleges all across the country. With those increased odds, I was bound to find a good fit sooner or later!

As luck would have it, my uncle is a United States Marine stationed near the college where I'll be attending. Not only will I have a great college experience, but I'll be able to see my aunt, uncle and cousins more often. If I had stayed close to home, I wouldn't have had that opportunity. It's funny how things work out in the end.

When Do I Start? How Do I Start?

Dad: $

I recommend that you start this process your freshman year in high school (ninth grade). College coaches are looking for recruits in all grades, focusing on juniors and seniors. However, an SA in ninth grade can be very focused on creating the habits they will use to succeed in their recruiting program.

If you are already past your 9th grade in high school, please don't worry. Even if you are a senior, you can still work through this process with success. It's not too late for you. You just have to shorten the time line on the activities that I list later in the book.

As I mentioned earlier, Emily was one of the lucky ones as she was14 years old and in 8th grade when she made the conscious decision to play softball at the college level. As we were driving home from practice one night, she told me she was going to write down her goals. I was glad when she showed it to me as I knew from past work experience that writing down goals was important. This very small act lets you see your goal as well as make it public. It greatly adds to your commitment.

Goal Setting:
Goal setting is a skill; just like throwing a softball correctly or swinging the bat to get a great hit. There is a right way and a wrong way to do it. The skill of goal setting is one that you can use in everything you do in life. That's right, everything you do... While I

could easily write another book on this subject alone, I will spend a few moments here giving you the basics so you can be successful.

There are two basic parts of goal setting.
1.) Writing the goal.
2.) Using the written goal to influence every decision you make.

Writing the Goal:
When writing a goal, I like to be smart about it. In fact, you can use the letters in the word **SMART**, to create an acronym to guide you through the goal setting process. **S.M.A.R.T.** refers to goals that are **S**pecific, **M**easurable, **A**chievable, **R**ealistic, and **T**imely.

Specific: Goals need to be specific. Goals are often set so loosely, it's nearly impossible to judge whether we hit them or not. For example, a statement like "I will bat better" is too vague. How will you know if and when you've reached your goal? Saying, " I will increase my batting average from .225 to .250 this month" is more specific. At the end of the month it will be easy to measure if you have increased your batting average to .250.

Measurable: Goals need to be measurable. For example, many of us want to increase our grade point average (GPA). But, "increasing our GPA" is not as clear as it could be. A clearer objective is "I will increase my GPA to a 4.0 on the next 4 exams by studying a minimum of 3 hours for each exam." You will know if you hit your goal by simply measuring the results.

Achievable: Goals need to be reasonable and achievable. All of us have wanted to improve our GPA. Often their success or failure depends on setting practical goals. Improving your GPA from a 3.0 to a 4.5 in one week is unrealistic. However, improving your GPA from a 3.0 to a 3.25 in one semester may be more reasonable. Don't set yourself up for failure by setting goals that are out of reach.

Realistic: Goals need to be realistic. It's important to honestly evaluate yourself. If you are a "slapper", a realistic goal may be to have a .300 batting average this season via all single – base hits. An unrealistic goal may be to expect to have 50% of your hits to be home runs. As a slapper, you normally wouldn't expect a home run so putting that into your goal may not be realistic.

Timely: Goals need to have a time frame; a beginning date and an end date. Having a set amount of time will give your goals structure. For example, you may want to improve your GPA so that more colleges will consider you for their softball program. If you spend time talking about what you want to do someday, but never act on it, your goal may never be realized. Without a beginning and end date there is no sense of urgency, no reason to take any action today. Having a specific time frame gives you a reason to get started. It also helps you monitor your progress as the end date gets closer.

Here's a sample goal that might help you to get started:

I will write an introductory e-mail to the 125 NCAA DII & DIII colleges on my existing college list. The e-mail will include my batting average, summer travel ball schedule, and a web link to my skills video, along with my name and telephone number. I will write at least ten e-mails every two days, until all the e-mails are sent (so it won't take me more than 25 days to complete this task). I will write one template e-mail and then copy and paste it to each college coach individually.

You can have more than one goal. Please take the time to write your SMART goal(s) here:

Date: _____

_____
_____
_____
_____
_____
_____
_____
_____
_____
_____
_____
_____
_____
_____
_____
_____
_____
_____
_____

Now photocopy this page and tape it to your mirror in your room or your bathroom. Read it out loud every time you look at it. I know it's really corny… but do it. When you read it out loud, it's <u>you</u> confirming what <u>you</u> want to do. No one has to be around to hear you say it. This is your promise to yourself.

Using the written Goal to Influence Every Decision You Make:

Writing a goal is only the first step. <u>Using</u> the goal is where the "rubber hits the road". Basically, a goal will be the guideline that you use when making decisions. Let me use an example to explain.

Using my sample goal above:
I will write an introductory e-mail to the 125 NCAA DII & DIII colleges on my existing college list. The e-mail will include my batting average, summer travel ball schedule, and a web link to my skills video, along with my name and telephone number. I will write at least ten e-mails every two days, until all the e-mails are sent (so it won't take me more than 25 days to complete this task). I will write one template e-mail and then copy and paste it to each college coach individually.

Let's say that I am on day number two after I've written this goal. My goal says I have to write ten e-mails every 2 days and I haven't written any yet. I just got home from softball practice after school, ate dinner and finished my homework. I get a call from my friend and she wants to go hang out at the mall with some other friends for an hour or so. I know if I do this, I'll never get my e-mails written and sent today as I will probably be too tired when I get home from the mall. So what do I do? Use the goal to answer your question. If you go to the mall today, will you accomplish your goal? The answer is obviously no. I'll reschedule with my friends and write the e-mails! It's an easy decision! It is easy to make these decisions once you have written SMART goals.

As you can see, when faced with a decision, just refer back to your goal and ask yourself this simple "yes" or "no" question. Will I accomplish my goal if I do this? If the answer is yes, then you are probably on the right track. If the answer is no, then why are you doing it?

Grades!

Dad: $

Many recruits overlook the most important part of their game. **<u>GRADES!</u>** They feel like if they run faster, throw harder, and hit the ball farther than everyone else, all of the colleges will be drooling over them. They could not be more wrong! You have to hit the books! Take the time in the first semester of your high school years to establish good study habits. Once you get a bad report card, you can never take it back. It is on your record forever. Damaging your grade point average (GPA) is not going to help you reach your goal. However, a good report card is one that will immediately get a college coach's attention. You may be the most gifted athlete in your sport, but if the admissions office can't accept you because of a poor GPA, then there is usually nothing that a coach can do for you. Look at it this way. If a coach isn't 100% confident that you will succeed academically at their college, why would they spend their scholarship dollars on you? A safer bet for that coach is with the SA that has the grades *and* the physical talent.

Go back to your goal that you just wrote. Please add the following sentence. If you are a freshman, sophomore, junior, or senior, it doesn't matter; write down a goal about getting a certain grade point average. For example, you can write "I will try to get a minimum of a _____ GPA this year of high school." Add the details of your SMART goal to make it specific, measurable, attainable, realistic, and timely. I don't care if you've never gotten an "A" in your life; add this to your goal. It is that important! Do not be afraid to push yourself. If you usually get B's, try to get A's. If you have a 3.5 now, try to get a 3.75. You don't have to be perfect, just try for improvement. Emily has a good story for you here.

Emily: ✒

The scholarship funds I was going to receive from my college were all set once I signed my National Letter of Intent. But I kept working on my grades anyway as I wanted to see how hard I could push myself my senior year of high school. The first semester resulted in a 4.5 GPA! It was one of my proudest moments ever. Not expecting anything to come of it, I sent my updated high school transcript to college. A couple of months later I received an additional $1000 / year in academic scholarship funds because it pushed me up into the next tier that the college had set up for granting these funds. I sure was glad that I didn't "coast" my senior year. The hard work really paid off!

The next several pages include your road map on how to use this book, a listing of what you will need to do and when you need to do it. Use it as your check list. As you complete each item, check it off on the calendar. You will get a great deal of satisfaction that comes with completing each step. Each time you check something, you are one step closer to living the dream!

How to Use this Book:

Dad: $

If you are picking up this book and starting the process after your freshman year in high school, it is ok. It is never too late to start working towards reaching your goal. You will just have to alter your time line a little bit. You can do it!

After you read the book most of your time will be spent in Chapter II, Chapter III, and Appendix A. I would like to clarify these three areas here:

What is Next in Chapter II?
Chapter II is the schedule or calendar for you from grades 9 – 12. You will see individualized check lists of when to complete each step while you are in high school. This is your calendar. It will help you to know <u>when</u> you should be completing specific tasks. Please go to Chapter II now to look it over. You will see many bullet/ boxes for you to check off as you complete each item on the calendar. You will also see some "steps" mentioned in some of the bullet/ boxes. I will explain the steps next as the steps are listed in Chapter III.

What is Next in Chapter III?
Step 1 through Step 9 are listed in Chapter III in detail. To clarify, the calendar in Chapter II simply tells you <u>when</u> you should be completing each step. The steps in Chapter III describe the specific actions that you will need to complete.

The steps in Chapter III are:

Step 1 - Visit the College Board, NCAA, NAIA, and NJCAA Web Sites
Step 2 - Creating a College List
Step 3 - Skills Video

Step 4 - Making Contact
Step 5 - Respond to Questionnaires and Other Inquiries
Step 6 - Visiting Colleges
Step 7 - The Application
Step 8 - The Offer - National Letter of Intent (NLI)
Step 9 - What Happens After I Sign?

Please go to Chapter III now to look it over. You will see Step 1 through Step 9 as mentioned in the calendar from Chapter II. Please go to Step 2. You'll see Appendix A mentioned in Step 2. I'll take some time here to talk about Appendix A.

Clarification of Appendix A

Appendix A is where you will document your list of colleges from Step 2. Step 2 is where you will spend quite a bit of time because you will be making a fairly large list in Appendix A the first time you complete this task. Once you read about Appendix A in Step 2, you will quickly know what to do as I will give you all the details there. Please go to Appendix A now to look it over. Right now it's just five lists with a lot of blank pages. Your job will be to fill those pages with the names of all the colleges that you may want to attend. As you work through this process, you will be shrinking your list smaller and smaller until you get to the final college where you will be attending.

Try to not get overwhelmed with the process. Did you ever hear the joke, "How do you eat an elephant?" The answer is; one bite at a time. This process is the same as the elephant. You can complete it one page at a time in this book! Just go to the next page and begin with Chapter II. The nice thing about this book is that Emily and I will walk you through the process in a very simple manner. Each step that you take gets you closer to living the dream of earning your softball scholarship!

Additional Resources:

If you need more help, want to contact the authors, and for additional services, please feel free to visit our web site!

www.mysoftballscholarship.com

Due to the possibility of date and deadline changes made by the NCAA, Emily and I have decided to leave out most of the specific deadline dates that were in place at the time this book was published. You will be searching their web site throughout the process so it is best to refer back to the most up-to-date information for dates and deadlines.

2
Schedule During Grades 9-12

The first step of the process is to determine where you are <u>in</u> the process. The first question you need to answer is this: What year of high school am I in? Easy enough, right? Now go to the next page and find your year of high school. **If you are a freshman or first year**, then you will be at the very beginning of the process. Notice how the various bullet/ boxes are listed here for your freshman year. Each bullet/box has a specific task for you to complete. Some bullet/boxes will tell you to go to a specific "Step" in Chapter III. If that is the case, then you have to go to Chapter III to get more information to complete that Step. For example, this is the second bullet/box item on the next page under, **"Freshman Year (9th Grade):"**

☐ PSAT – See Step 1 in the Chapter III and find the link to the College Board Tests. The PSAT is a practice run for the SAT. Register and take the PSAT test.

When you get to this bullet/box, you will then go the Chapter III to complete Step 1 because it tells you to do this. After you have completed Step 1 in Chapter III, return to your calendar to place a check mark "√" in the box. That way you will know that you have completed this bullet/box and can visit the next bullet/box. Obviously you will not be able to complete all the bullet/boxes in one day. Just take one at a time and complete them within the year they correspond with your high school year. If you get them out of order, that will be ok too. Just try to complete them in the order that makes sense to you, your schedule, and your personal situation.

If you are a sophomore, junior or senior and just picking up this book, please don't be concerned. You just have some "make-up" work to complete. With any luck, you may have already completed some of the bullet/boxes already. To be safe, go to the calendar and start with the freshman year bullet/boxes and make sure you have completed them all. Check off each bullet/box until you get to the year that you are currently attending at your high school. In your case, you will most definitely be completing many of the items out-of-order. Please do not let this concern you. It will be necessary to complete the bullet/boxes out-of-order so you can complete them in a timely fashion.

You are probably getting tired of hearing the words bullet and box by now... Can you say "bullet box" three times fast? ☺ I thought so! Go to the schedule below and start the process with the first bullet/box.

Schedule during Grades 9 – 12:

Freshman Year (9ᵗʰ Grade):

☐ This is the best year to establish good study habits as your classes will get a little harder next year. Study, Study, Study... Your main focus should be your grades right now!

☐ PSAT – See Step 1 in the Chapter III and find the link to the College Board Tests. The PSAT is a practice run for the SAT. Register and take the PSAT test.

☐ Find Step 1 (again) in Chapter III to get familiar with the process. Jump on-line and start looking at colleges. *Note to Parents: If you are not computer savvy, don't panic! Your SA probably is computer savvy. What a great opportunity to bond with your daughter while learning a little about computers!*

☐ Find Step 2 in Chapter III to get familiar with the process. You can start to work on your college list if you like, but it is not critical in your freshman year. You will see it again in your sophomore year of high school (next year).

☐ Clean up your act... Google your name on-line. A prospective coach will do this so you need to know what they will see. Do you have crazy pictures or videos on myspace, youtube, facebook, or any other web site that reflect on you in a poor light? Delete anything that is remotely questionable. Check out the privacy settings to control content on your page.

☐ Enjoy your sport, play hard!

Sophomore Year (10th Grade):

- ☐ Complete Step 1 in Chapter III.
- ☐ Complete Step 2 in Chapter III .
- ☐ Complete Step 3 in Chapter III.
- ☐ Complete Step 4 in Chapter III.
  A schedule of your travel team's tournaments and show cases should accompany each e-mail, inviting the coach to all events. The coach might not respond to you yet so just include the invitation to all coaches that you send the e-mail. A sample e-mail is included for you in Step 4.
- ☐ Complete Step 5 in Chapter III as applicable
- ☐ Continue to Study, Study, Study…
- ☐ Continue to enjoy your sport!

Junior Year (11th Grade):

- ☐ Take the SAT or ACT in the fall of your junior year.
  SAT - http://www.collegeboard.com/
  ACT - http://www.act.org/
  You can take them multiple times and should plan on doing so. Your score will usually improve the second time you take these standardized tests.
- ☐ Visit with your high school guidance counselor for tips and possible practice sessions for the SAT/ACT.
- ☐ You may have to take the SAT II Subject Tests depending on your target colleges and course study. Ask your high school counselor about this.
- ☐ Revisit Step 1 - NCAA Clearinghouse: Sign up if you haven't done so already. http://eligibilitycenter.org
- ☐ Revisit Step 2 – Make additions & deletions to your college list.
- ☐ Tell all your coaches which colleges you are interested in and ask for their help in this process. Show them this outline so they know the process you are following.
- ☐ Revisit Step 3 – If your skill level has improved, you may need to create a new skills video.
- ☐ Revisit Step 4 – Contact all colleges again via e-mail with this year's schedule of events, games, tournaments, show cases, etc. A schedule of your travel team's tournaments and show cases should accompany each e-mail, inviting the coach to all events. The coach might not respond to you yet so just include the invitation to all coaches to whom you send the e-mail. A sample e-mail is included in the book at Step 4.
- ☐ Complete Step 5 as applicable

☐ If you have completed your junior year in high school and it is after July 1, feel free to call the college coach directly via telephone and invite him/her to your events. Don't be shy here. Many SA's will not take this important step because they are nervous, scared, or don't think that they are allowed to do it. Practice with a parent or coach before you call if you feel nervous. Role play by using your cell phone so it's really on the phone for a real life practice experience. Write down a brief script that you can read in case you get the coach's voice mail. That way you will sound mature and professional.

You wouldn't play your sport without practicing first so why should this very important telephone contact be any different? It is all part of the game! Step up and make the call… It may be the call that changes your life forever.

☐ Google your name on-line again before the end of your junior year, before July 1. Clean up any items you see that may be a problem for a college coach or your recruiting process in general.

☐ Complete Step 6. Try to visit any colleges that are high on your list. If you are traveling, try to keep an informal college visit in mind when making your travel plans. If you do visit a college, e-mail the coach and let him/her know you are coming. They should already have your name from your previous contacts.

☐ If you cannot visit the college, try a virtual tour of the college on line. Not all schools have it, but if they do, it is a great tool to review. Most schools, however, have a web site with all their information on it.

☐ Review Step 7.

☐ Review Step 8.

☐ Review Step 9.

Senior Year (12th Grade):

☐ Revisit Step 1 - NCAA Clearinghouse: Sign up if you haven't done so already. http://eligibilitycenter.org

   o Send your high school transcripts (list of classes taken and grades) to the NCAA Clearinghouse.

   o Send your SAT/ACT scores to the NCAA Clearinghouse.

☐ Visit with your high school guidance counselor for tips and possible practice sessions for the SAT/ACT.

☐ Take the SAT or ACT again in the fall of your senior year.

SAT - http://www.collegeboard.com/

ACT - http://www.act.org/

☐ Revisit Step 2 – Make additions & deletions to your college list. Your list should start to shrink now. You want to start to focus on specific colleges that either you would like to attend, or colleges that have shown an interest in you. I call this the short list. Strive to get your list down to about 5 or 6 colleges now.

☐ Tell all your current coaches which colleges you are really interested in and ask for their help in this process. Show them this book again so they know the process you are following. Share your short list with your coach. Tell your coach which colleges are contacting you. Communication is key! You have come this far. You do not want to miss anything now.

☐ Revisit Step 4 – Contact all colleges again via e-mail with this year's schedule of events, games, tournaments, show cases, etc. A schedule of your travel team's summer tournaments and show case events should accompany each e-mail, inviting the coach to all events. This should not be as difficult of a task since your college list is much shorter than before. The college coach should be responding to you so you should be communicating directly with coaches on your list.

☐ Complete Step 5 as applicable

☐ Complete Step 6. If you haven't done so already, you should visit as many colleges as possible now! You do not want to make a choice unless you have physically visited the college campus and spoken to the coach in person. E-mail the coach and schedule an appointment with them. They should already have your name from your previous contacts.

☐ Review Step 7.

☐ Review Step 8.

☐ Review Step 9.

3

Steps To Success

Dad: $

Step 1: Visit the College Board, NCAA, NAIA, and NJCAA Web Sites

Familiarizing yourself with the tools that you will be using is where we will start the process. In order to keep this information relevant and up-to-date, I am going to refer you to the web site where the source information is kept. You'll be looking at the web sites for the College Board, NCAA, NAIA, and NJCAA. I will explain each one for you.

College Board:
http://www.collegeboard.com
The College Board web site is a place where you will spend a lot of time. It is a "must have" resource and I think it's a great place to start. This is where you will register to take the College Board Tests (SAT). It will also help you plan for college, look for a college, apply to a college and even help you figure out how to pay for college. Through a series of Q and A on the "Find a College" tab, the site will help you to find all colleges across the country that may be a potential fit for your specific needs. Through a series of questions and answers, you'll be able to filter out colleges that you are not interested in. For example, it will specify what part of the country you would like to be in, Division I,

II, or III, topic of study you wish to pursue, and many more. What will be left at the end of the Q&A will be a list of colleges that may be a good fit for you. You can create a user name and password so you can save your searches, revisit them later, revise them, etc. It is a good way to stay organized too.

College Board Sign-In Information:

User Name:_____

Password:_____

NCAA Eligibility Center - National Collegiate Athletic Association
http://eligibilitycenter.org
You will have to come here sooner or later to register with the NCAA so now is a good time. This is also another great tool for you. First things first; what is the NCAA? The NCAA is The National Collegiate Athletic Association. It's a non-profit organization. Its members are a diverse group and are located all over the country – including over 1200 colleges and universities, conferences and other organizations. You can click on the explanations on this site to learn more about the NCAA and the difference between Divisions I, II, and III.

In this section, you will be able to register yourself with the NCAA and find all the colleges and universities that participate in the NCAA.

NCAA Eligibility Center Sign-In Information:

User Name:_____

Password:_____

Click on the appropriate places and get yourself registered with the NCAA. Write down your user name and password here so you have it for later. Once you are in the site, surf around a little bit so you know what is here. This site is interactive so have some fun with it. You can find the place (the whistle) that lists all sports and then it breaks it down by Division I, II, & III colleges. This resource is worth its weight in gold as each institution and conference has links to their respective web sites. You can also sort each category here. It will save you countless hours if you learn to use this site early in your search.

NAIA – National Association of Intercollegiate Athletics
NAIA and NJCAA (Junior Colleges) may also be your target. You won't find them listed on the NCAA web page as they are not part of the NCAA. As of 2008, the NAIA has 287 member institutions and the NJCAA had 525 member colleges for the 2009-2010 academic years so don't forget to check out the NAIA and NJCAA too! You will find many really good schools here. I said it before and I'll say it again…

> **"The larger the net you cast, the more fish you will catch!"**

Here is the link to the official NAIA site that lists all the NAIA colleges in the USA:
http://naia.cstv.com/

Nearly 300 member institutions make up the National Association of Intercollegiate Athletics (NAIA). These colleges and universities can be found throughout the United States and Canada and are divided into 25 different conferences!

NJCAA – National Junior College Athletic Association
Below is the link to a list of all Junior Colleges in the USA (NJCAA):
http://www.njcaa.org/

The National Junior College Athletic Association (NJCAA) is the governing body of intercollegiate athletics for two-year colleges so their web site is a great place to visit. Its programs are designed to meet the unique needs of a diverse group of student-athletes who come from both traditional and non-traditional backgrounds.

Junior colleges provide an excellent stepping stone to get you to the dream 4 year university or college of your choice. You can spend the two years while you are in a junior college to prepare yourself physically and mentally for a college that offers a four year program. Many junior colleges offer scholarship opportunities too!

Notes:

Step 2

Dad: $

Creating a College List

Once you have completed Step 1, you will want to visit each college's web site to check them out. Use the web sites in Step 1 to create the list of schools that best fits your specific needs. You can list any information from the colleges that you select here. If you are not sure about any college, leave it <u>on</u> the list. It is better to have your list too big vs. too small at this stage of the process.

In Appendix A, I recommend you set up your list of colleges in five different categories. These categories are:

- **Reach Schools**
- **Attainable Schools**
- **Safety Schools**
- **Other/Maybe**
- **Coach Contacted Me But Not On My List**

Please go to Appendix A now to see how the list is set up.

For those of you that are more tech-savvy, you can mark each college under "Favorites" on your web browser. If you start to make favorite files on your computer, I would strongly recommend that you store them in various folders on your computer to help you stay organized. You can still break your list down further in terms of DII, DIII, state, or city but break them down in the five main categories first.

Student Athletes; if your parents are not as tech-savvy as you are, be patient with them. Take some time to explain this information to them. Remember, this is a team effort!

Reach Schools:

A reach school is a college or university that may be a little bit out of reach for you in terms of grades, standardized test scores, finances, or athletic ability. Recognizing a college as a reach school is healthy in that you know that your chances of getting accepted academically or athletically may be some what low. However, list them here anyway because if you don't try, you definitely will not have the opportunity to attend.

Attainable Schools:
An attainable school is where the bulk of your list should be. It is one where your grades, standardized test scores, finances, or athletic ability fall within the college's current guidelines. In other words, you are a person that this school is looking for and vice-versa; this is a school that "you" are looking for!

Safety Schools:
A safety school list should be relatively short. This is a list of colleges that you know you will easily be accepted. This is what I call "Plan B". You always want to keep a few safety schools on your list just in case you don't get accepted into the college of your dreams.

Other/Maybe:
This is a "catch all" college list. You don't know where else to put it so you are just parking it here until you either put in on your Reach / Attainable / Safety list or drop it off your list all together.

Coach Contacted Me But Not On My List:
This is an exciting list to have and one of my favorites! Imagine you are checking your e-mail one day and out of the blue a college coach e-mails you and tells you they are interested in you. You go to your list to check them out and they are not even on your list. WOW! These are opportunities that most likely came to you from a show case event or perhaps word of mouth. Either way, you want to certainly pay attention to these contacts and add them to your list. Even after you research the college and learn it is not really what you wanted, this might become a college for your Safety School list.

"The larger the net you cast, the more fish you will catch!"

Emily:

After I completed this step, I took the time to review it with my parents. They had a few good comments about colleges that I had on my list. They also recommended some colleges that weren't on my list that I should consider adding to the list. My mom used to be a college recruiter before becoming a teacher so she knows a lot about colleges across the country. She was a really good resource for me in this part of the process. You can also ask your high school counselor, teachers, or coaches about the colleges you have on your list. School counselors and teachers will have a college degree so they might be able to give you some guidance in this area. The bottom line is that it doesn't hurt to keep your list too big.

This is where you will list the colleges you are interested in: (If the list is too big to write down, then just print it from your computer and keep a copy of the list in Appendix A for future reference. Date the list so you can track changes.) Appendix A is where you can write down all of your colleges. I've already broken the list down for you into the five categories in Appendix A:

- **Reach Schools**
- **Attainable Schools**
- **Safety Schools**
- **Other/Maybe**
- **Coach Contacted Me But Not On My List**

All you have to do is put the school in the proper category. Please go to Appendix A now to complete your list. Don't be surprised if this takes you a few attempts to complete the list. I worked on this step for several weeks.

Step 3 – Skills Video

Dad: $

Lights, Action, Camera....!   While you are working on gathering your list of colleges, you should also be creating your skills video. You can talk with your coach for some people/companies in your area who can create this important tool for you or you can ask a relative or friend to do it for you if they have a video camera. This one item will often get your foot in the door and get the attention from the college coaches you are seeking to talk to (after they look at your grades). Below are the actual skills videos Emily made and sent to colleges:

http://www.youtube.com/watch?v=WMbjHTGVwAg

http://www.youtube.com/watch?v=k60cad6rnwY

The specific items you will want to include in your skills video are as follows:

- You introducing yourself (briefly) and thanking the viewer for watching your skills video.
- You playing your specific defensive position(s) (alone on the field).
  - o If outfield, you should be seen taking fly/ground balls and throwing them to a cut-off person in the infield.
  - o If infield, you should be seen taking mostly ground balls and throwing them to first. However, mix up the tape with a line drive, pop-fly or turning a double play if applicable.

o If a pitcher, you will want to show pitching plus defensive skills if you play two positions. You can have a batter present but it is not necessary. Pitch speed can be shown but try to show ball movement. Show pitching technique from four angles around you.

o If a catcher, you will want to show yourself catching all types of pitches (grounders in the dirt, inside, outside, up, down, etc). Show footwork and blocking skills, and throw downs to second (glove to glove time). Show catching technique from four angles around you.

o If you play multiple positions, show them all. Players who play multiple positions may give a college coach more opportunities to fit you into their lineup.

- You batting from a pitching machine. No catcher in the frame.
  o If you bat as a right and left hander, show both.
  o If you are a slapper, show slapping and hitting.
  o Show bunting.
- You running down to first base after a hit. No other players should be in the frame.
- Your tape should be as brief as possible. Just show your skills as listed above and then stop. Two or three minutes should be enough to show your skills.

What not to show in your skills tape:

- You standing around in a game setting with your uniform on. You do not need to be wearing a uniform for the tape. The coach will not care.
- You sitting on the bench.
- You goofing around with your friends.
- Your house, your family, your pets, your extracurricular activities.
- A full infield and outfield on the field during the taping. You should be the only person on the field while taping, with the exception of the person feeding the pitching machine, or the person who is catching your thrown softball to demonstrate accuracy.
- You hitting a home run with every pitch thrown. Home runs are great, but a coach will know when you have edited out all your other hits. This may display a character flaw of dishonesty which may negatively affect your chances at a college.
- You or someone else yelling, swearing, or saying anything negative in reaction to a great play that someone caught on video tape. It's ok to show a great play if it demonstrates your skill level, just remove the sound if anything questionable is present.
- You talking about how great you play or how badly you want to go to a specific college. (Let your skills video do the talking for you. A brief "hello" and "thank you" is the only thing you should say.)
- A poorly lighted area where it is hard to see due to darkness or a camera pointed directly into the sunlight showing a lot of glare.

- An image where it is difficult to tell who the player is. There should be no question that the person on the tape is you.

Post your video on www.youtube.com. It's free and easy! Or, you can see your coach about hiring a local company that will post your video for a fee. I am a firm believer that you can post this information without paying for it. It will usually cost you some money to have the video created if you hire a professional. But why pay to create it and put it on line if you don't have to? You are going to send the link directly to the coaches so you do not have to worry about leaving it to fate for someone to see it. Most web sites that post skills videos also claim that they will get it noticed by college coaches.

The approach I'm recommending in this process is for you to do the work yourself.

Doing things yourself will save money while developing your relationship with the coach. I feel that it is far more personal and it allows you, the SA to own the process. You will care more about it and be far more involved in it if you do it yourself.

The best time to schedule the filming of your skills video is during your sophomore and/or junior year. Since you will want to start getting your videos out in your sophomore year, I recommend completing 2 videos. One in your sophomore year and then another in your junior year. If your first video turns out great, then you might not need another one. But I've found that there is a great deal of athletic development happening with teens between the ages of 15 – 18 so your game may improve significantly in that time frame. If it does, you will want the college coaches to see it!

I have seen some girls get their video filmed and edited professionally. But if you have little money to spend on the skills video, do not be afraid to make it yourself or ask a friend with a video camera to help out.

If a college coach is interested in you, they may play your video several times. First impressions are critical. I have seen plenty of good skill videos completed by amateur videographers like parents, relatives, etc. Another good source of videographers is your local high school camera crew. They may be looking for a project. Just try to get the best video you can that shows you and your skills in the best light.

Emily:

I know plenty of girls who made their skills video on their own. Many of these girls ended up at really good colleges. Some even got full scholarships at DI schools. If you think you don't have the time or money to pay for a skills video, don't think that you won't have a good chance to get into college because of this one thing. Do what works best for you! Just be sure the video demonstrates your skill and athleticism. Try to work really hard during filming so you show the college coaches what you're all about. Lastly, if you do the video yourself, don't worry about putting music on it in the background. I've had a few college coaches tell me that the music is a distraction. Most of them turn the volume down anyway so it's really a waste of time and effort to put music on it. The coaches are looking at it to see your skill level, not to listen to music.

Dad:

You may want to follow-up with a phone call or e-mail within a few weeks after sending your video to confirm that they received it. At the very least, it's important for the coaches to receive your video in May and June of your junior year in high school so that they can watch you play in a tournament before July 1.

Step 4 - Making Contact:

Dad:

Now that you have a list of colleges, it is time to let them know that you are thinking about them. This is where you are going to spend some time and effort. Emily found success with e-mailing every single college coach that she was interested in. She e-mailed every DIII and almost every DII college on her list. The college she eventually signed with was one of the last ones that she e-mailed. If she had stopped before she finished her list, this college would have never known Emily's name. My point is this; once you make this list, you have to commit to sticking with this process until you manage the list down to the one school where you will attend. You will constantly be adding and subtracting school names throughout the process. This is where your "sweat equity" comes in. **You have to do the work in Step 4!** You Can Do It!

Here's what I recommend (in chronological order) to save some time on this step:

- First you want to write a generic e-mail that you can use for all coaches. Once you have it written, you can easily cut and paste it to all coaches. I would strongly recommend that you send one individual e-mail to each coach. Do not send a broadcast e-mail to multiple coaches at the same time or blind copy others on your e-mail. It takes more time this way, but it is a more individualized and personal approach. A sample e-mail is listed at the end of this section.

Include the following:

- o An introduction explaining who you are and why you are contacting them. Be as brief as possible, as coaches are busy.

- o A link to your recruiting video if you have one – Post it on **www.youtube.com** as it is free.

- o A recruiting resume with details such as stats, honors, academic data and contact information for your high school and club coaches. Refer to the Player Profile on page 46. You can use the Player Profile as a template. Your resume doesn't have to look just like the Player Profile. If you want to change it, feel free. But it should have the same basic information in it. Be honest here. Don't embellish data. If you are weak in a certain area, it is better to leave it off than to fabricate information. Embellishing the truth is a character flaw that most coaches will not tolerate.

> ## When in doubt, leave it out!

Some times when gathering the information for this task, it can be a little overwhelming. If you were not in the habit of keeping your own stats, you might want to visit the MaxPreps web site. MaxPreps is the site where many high schools report their player's statistics.

www.maxpreps.com
Take a minute and log into this site to see what your high school coach has submitted. These stats tend to become a matter of record so check their accuracy to make sure they accurately reflect you and your athletic accomplishments. You can use these stats to show the college coaches what your athletic experiences have been. It's a great tool.

Emily:

After all the practices, games, and show case tournaments that I played in, the thing that actually got me in front of the college where I signed and got my scholarship was an e-mail with my skills video link attached to it. I learned that the reason my dad asked me to send so many e-mails was that it was increasing my chances to get my name and video in front of college coaches that might need the skills that I had to offer. The summer between my junior and senior year, I e-mailed over 200 coaches. I know, it sounds like a ridiculous number of e-mails. But I only had to do a few every day and it didn't take long at all. I already had my list of colleges handy and I just used the same e-mail over (sample on next page) and over for each college. Once the e-mail was written, the actual 200 e-mails were easy.

A strategy that I used to make this task a little simpler was this. I would try to knock out at least 10 or more e-mails each day. I found that if I broke it down to just 10 each day, I could do it and it was easier to think about. If I thought about doing all 200, I would be overwhelmed and not do anything.

> **Break a big job down into smaller tasks so it is easier to do!**

Here's a sample e-mail that I used. You don't have to write a long e-mail. Keep it brief. Feel free to use this one but type in your personal experiences in place of mine.

Hi Coach Jones,

My name is (your name here) and I play for (club or travel team name here). I am a (team position(s) listed here) from (High School name here) in (town & state name here) graduating with the class of (graduating year here). (List other points of interest here that may set you apart from other players.) Example: A few weeks ago I was invited to play with an ASA women's open team, where I got the chance to play against the Australian National Team. Now that their season has ended, I have returned to my travel team where I will begin the fall season with showcases and tournaments. I have an overall GPA of (grade point average here) and intend on going to a four-year college/university. I would appreciate it if you could take a look at my skills video on (skills video link here). If you have any questions, please feel free to e-mail or call me. I hope to hear from you soon!

(Your Name Here)
(Your Phone Number Here)

Show Case Events:

Dad: $

Show Case Events are where the idea of this book was born. These are events held specifically for showcasing your talents to college coaches. See your coach about times, places, and your personal participation. Once you learn where and when they take place, and if you are invited, you can usually go on line to see which colleges will be attending.

The reason that this is in Step 4 is because it is often the first time that a college coach may see you play. I consider it a very important contact so it is in the "Making Contact" section. As I stated earlier in this book, I am a typical parent and I spoke to many other parents while watching Emily play softball. I could not believe how many SA's and parents that I spoke with at showcase events who did not think to invite a college coach to watch them perform.

This is a critical step and must not be missed.

The reason you are playing at a showcase event is to be seen by a college coach!

That is why these events are held. To simply show up and pray that some random coach will see you is not utilizing this opportunity to its fullest extent.

You will want to compare your list of prospective colleges from Step 2 with the on-line list from the showcase or college invitational tournaments that you attend. If the list isn't posted on line, ask your coach for a list of colleges who will be attending. Then you can simply send out invitations via e-mail to your prospective college coaches. Keep in mind that NCAA rules prohibit college coaches from calling high school athletes until after their junior year (July1). However, there is no rule prohibiting you from contacting the coach. So invite any coach that you wish. Just don't expect them to respond. **Chances are, they may see you there and you may not even know it unless they reveal themselves to your coach.** That is very normal. Because you may not know who they are, you will want to read the next page; items #1 - #4 very carefully.

There are some basic rules that you must follow while attending a showcase event.

#1. Assume that a college coach is watching you every minute of every day, on and off the field. Assume they see you at the hotel at night, while you are sitting on the bench, and while you are getting snacks at the snack bar. Act accordingly. Remember why you are here. If your coach has not instructed the team about this topic, ask your coach if they are going to address the team about their behavior on and off the field. Your coach will be impressed that you are thinking about it. But more importantly, it will communicate this message to the rest of your team so that all of your teammates are on the same page with respect to your coach's expectations surrounding their behavior at the tournament.

#2. While you are playing at the showcase event, don't be surprised if a college coach asks to see you play a position other than where your current coach plays you. They may want to see you play a certain position but only have a few minutes to watch before moving on to their next prospect. They may ask your coach to switch your position right in the middle of an inning. This is a good thing, not a bad thing. It means they are interested in you. So do not hang your head or throw a hissy fit. With a smile on your face, quickly move to the new position. They may also ask you to bat 2 or 3 times in a row in the same inning. Sounds crazy, I know, but it happens. In a showcase tournament, there are no rules against this as the main objective of the showcase tournament is to allow college coaches to observe prospective SA's in action. Sometimes it takes more than one "at bat" for them to properly evaluate you in the limited time they have to observe you.

#3. Speak with your coach before the showcase tournament. Let him/her know who you have invited. Also ask him/her that if a college coach presents themselves to him/her, to please let you know about it after the game. This is important so that you can send an e-mail to them thanking them for coming to see you. Many SA's miss this important step and it will help separate you from your competition.

This is important so that you can send an e-mail to the coach thanking them for coming to see you.

Many SA's miss this important step and it will help separate you from your competition.

#4. **Player Profile:** Many SA's create player profiles to give to college coaches during the showcase tournaments. Player Profiles allow a college coach to get information about a player on the spot. This is a great tool, especially if a coach is in a hurry and not able to see you but wants to circle back to you later, either at the tournament or afterward via e-mail, they can use this as a reminder. The next page is an example of what a sample player profile might look like. You can use this as a template if you like.

Sample Player Profile Template (next page):

TEAM NAME
18U Girls Fast Pitch Softball
Manager Name Here; (951) 555-1212, coach_name@yahoo.com
http://eteamz.active.com/teamname/

Your Name Here
Date of Birth: ##/##/####
Height: 5'10"
Weight: 170 lbs

Insert Player Picture and Jersey # Here

ATHLETIC:
Position(s) Played: Catcher & Outfield
Throw: R Hit: R

ATHLETIC:
Position(s) Played: Catcher/ Outfield
Throw: R Hit: R

TRAVEL SOFTBALL EXPERIENCE:

Team Name 20## - 20##: Coach Name
Team Name 20## - 20##: Coach Name
Team Name 20## - 20##: Coach Name
Team Name 20## - 20##: Coach Name

SOFTBALL TEAM ACCOMPLISHMENTS:

Little League Regional Champions 20##
Little League State Champions 20##
Little League District Champions 20##
Undefeated ASA National Qualifier (Lakeland, Florida 20##)
7th Place at ASA Nationals 20##
.333 Batting Average for last 3 years
High School Team Co-Captain – Senior Year

HOME ADDRESS: 123 Any Street, Town Name, State 12345

Parents: Softball Mom & Softball Dad

E-mail: e-mail address here

ACADEMIC:
Class of 20##
High School: High School Name Here

High School Coach: Coach Name Here (coach e-mail address here)

Grade: 12th

GPA: 4.25
SAT Score: 1450
Honor Roll: Yes

HIGH SCHOOL EXPERIENCE:

Freshmen Year: Freshmen Team
Sophomore Year: Varsity Team
Junior Year: Varsity Team
Senior Year: Varsity Team

OTHER ACTIVITES/INTEREST

High School Drum Line
Professional Percussionist
Invisible Children Club
Mission Work in Mexico
Author

College Clinics:

Dad: $

As always there are exceptions to every rule. One way you can expose your talents to college coaches without violating NCAA rules is by attending clinics that colleges put on for your sport. College teams often hold fund raising clinics in order to earn money for their team expenses. They do this by holding training clinics to teach skills to anyone who wishes to attend. Sometimes these events are by invitation only but other times they will open up the clinic to anyone. Attending one of these events can allow you to visit a campus and meet the coach and team in a setting that allows you to demonstrate your skill level. These events are usually held at the college campus so it allows you to visit the campus at the same time. It's a great way to get some work in on your skills while trying to figure out if you like the college atmosphere and geographic area of the college you are visiting.

Step 5 – Respond to Questionnaires and Other Inquiries:

Dad: $

College Coaches will commonly place your name on an automated "tickler" system or "drip campaign" that sends out information about their program and college automatically every month or so if it is after July 1 and you have completed your junior year in high school. It is how the coach may keep track of you. In order to get your name on their list, most colleges will have "Questionnaires" posted on their web sites. If a coach sends you an e-mail in response to your e-mail from Step 4, promptly go in and complete the questionnaire. If you delay in completing the questionnaire, the coach may take it as a sign that you are not interested, are lazy, or just do not care. Be careful not to give a coach a reason to remove your name from their list of potential recruits.

If a college coach responds to your e-mail, it is a great time to acknowledge the coach by returning his e-mail with a nice "Thank you" e-mail. It gives you the opportunity to begin developing a relationship with the coach and show them why you will be a great addition to their team and sports program. If you have any upcoming events, an updated video, or something special that happened to you (academically or athletically), it is also a good time to let the coach know about these items.

At this stage of the game, you will probably start to receive many letters in the mail from many different colleges. The College Board web site and your high school may have shared your information with some of these colleges if you fit within their target profile. In other words, you might receive a letter from a college that was not on your list. However, your grades and SAT scores may fall within that particular college's target profile. You are the type of student they are looking for! You may want to take a second look at their web sites when you receive their letters. You never know what you might find.

The following is a copy of an e-mail trail for you to get an idea of what you might expect to see. *The names and places have been changed to protect the identity of the coach and college.* What started out as a drip campaign from one college ended up with Emily scheduling a visit to this particular school.

From: College Coach
To: Emily Poulton
Subject: College Softball

Hi Emily,

This is Coach Jones, the new head coach at ABC College in Pittsburgh, PA. I know you had expressed some previous interest in ABC College so I am contacting you to see if you are still interested. If you are, or have any questions for me, please e-mail me! Also, if you have a skills video to send me that would be great.

Thanks Emily and I hope to hear from you soon!

Coach Jones

Anna Jones
ABC College
Head Softball Coach
Pittsburgh, PA 92651
(860) 123-4567

From: Emily Poulton
To: College Coach
Subject: College Softball

Hey Coach Jones,

Thank you very much for introducing yourself. During my spring break, I took a trip through PA to look at colleges in that area and I stopped by ABC College to watch a game. I got a chance to look around the campus and enjoyed my time in the area. It is a wonderful little town and I felt very comfortable there.

I am looking for a private college on the East Coast and with an outstanding reputation. ABC College is at the top of my list! I would appreciate it if you could check out my skills video which is posted on YouTube; here is the link:
http://www.youtube.com/watch?v=WMbjHTGVwAg

Thank you again for the introduction and I look forward to talking to you in the future!

Emily Poulton

From: College Coach
To: Emily Poulton
Subject: College Softball

Hi Emily,

That is great that ABC is still at the top of your list and it is also great that you have already had a chance to come to campus and see a game. After watching your video, I know you could contribute to our program. We are looking for another catcher (right now we only have one)...your arm looks great and you look quick behind the plate. I also think your swing looks very fundamentally sound.

Have you taken any honors/AP courses at your HS or do you plan to next year?

I know you are out in CA and it probably won't be easy for you to get back to the east coast soon, but we are hosting a recruiting weekend Oct. 18th/19th on campus. Would it be at all possible for you to come and do an overnight?

Let me know what you think,
Coach Jones

From: Emily Poulton
To: College Coach
Subject: College Softball

Hey Coach Jones,

Thank you very much for taking the time to view my skills video. To answer your question, I have taken a total of five AP classes; my school does not offer honors courses. This fall I am scheduled to take AP Government, AP Calculus BC, AP Spanish, and possibly AP English or AP Psychology.

As far as traveling goes, my older sister attends UMASS, Amherst and my family and I had already discussed a fall visit to your area. It just so happens that UMASS homecoming is that weekend and my parents had already planned our trip for those dates. In short, an overnight visit at ABC that weekend sounds great!

Lastly, I have attached an unofficial transcript and a copy of my last report card for you to view.

Hope to hear from you soon!

Emily Poulton

From: College Coach
To: Emily Poulton
Subject: College Softball

Hi Emily,

I am so happy that weekend works for you and your family! Academically and athletically you seem like a great fit for ABC College. Good luck with the remainder of your summer season. Keep in touch and plan on coming to ABC on October 18th!

Coach Jones

From: Jeff Poulton
To: College Coach
Subject: College Softball

Hi Coach. I wanted to send you a quick e-mail about Emily. We taped some of her play when her ASA Women's Open team played the Australian National Team this past summer directly after Australia lost to Team USA in Oklahoma. It was quite a thrill to see Emily play at that level. We posted it on you tube so you can watch it. We're looking forward to seeing you in October. Until then…

Here's the link…

http://www.youtube.com/watch?v=k60cad6rnwY

Jeff Poulton

Note to Parents: As you can see in these e-mails, keeping up the communication is key to your SA's success. It is ok for a parent or guardian to put in a "brag" e-mail to the coach now and again. But for the most part, the SA should be the one doing the majority of the communicating with the college coach. The coach is recruiting the SA, not the parent!

Things are Heating Up Now!

Dad: $

If college coaches are responding to you, then you are probably at the stage where the NCAA rules allow them to start to communicate with you directly. As stated in Step 5, many coaches will have opted to put your name and e-mail address on what we call a "drip campaign". A drip campaign is an automated e-mail campaign that "drips" on you like a leaky faucet drips water into the sink. E-mails are sent to you at a designated interval (weekly, bi-weekly, or monthly) in an effort to keep in touch with you and to keep their college's name in front of you throughout the recruiting process. Some coaches like these because they can enter your name into their database and more-or-less forget about you for a while because the e-mails are sent automatically. From your perspective, you see e-mails from a college coach so it keeps you interested in them. Just know that it's a common recruiting technique that coaches' use so they can maximize their time spent recruiting with as little effort as possible.

Here is a sample of a drip e-mail: *(again, the name of the college was removed)*

Dear Emily,
We are so excited that your summer is going well! When considering a great education we want to make you aware of where XYZ University currently ranks.

1. Department of Biomedical engineering is ranked 2nd in nation.

2. XYZ Law School is ranked 18th in nation.

3. XYZ School of Medicine is ranked 2nd in nation.

4. XYZ Business School is ranked 4th in nation.

5. XYZ School of Public Health is rated 5th in nation.

The above is just the beginning!

Oh, and don't forget our XYZ Softball Team!

Emily:

This reminds me of a really good DIII school in the south eastern part of the country that saw me at the Sparkler Showcase in Colorado. They immediately put me on their drip campaign after the tournament. It was my first one so I was really excited. They sent the e-mails to my travel ball coach who would forward them on to me. I was in my junior year of high school that year so it was cool to know that someone was interested in me. As time went on and I started to communicate more with the coach, I learned that they weren't as interested in me as I had originally thought. Because I was getting so many e-mails from the drip campaign, I thought they really wanted me. They eventually invited me to be on the team as a walk on. This was disappointing but it helped me learn to be careful about putting all my eggs into one basket. It taught me to be sure to continue the process and keep looking at all the potential colleges until I was actually signed with one of them. It's definitely a process and not a one time event.

While I'm thinking about coaches communicating with me, I also want to take a moment here to talk about answering the telephone during the recruiting process. Coaches will call you on your cell phone if you provide your number. They called me all the time. At first I was nervous about what to say or not say. But I learned that if I wasn't in a place where I could speak with them at that very second, it was best to be honest and ask if it was ok for me to call them back later. I never had a coach get mad at me for this. You might think that you have to give an answer to every question when they call you. But they understand that you have other things going on in your life.

One time I was at an important appointment when a college coach called. It definitely wasn't a good time to talk so I just asked the coach if I could call back later. She was fine with that. I called her back later and found out she was calling to offer me a position on her team! What that taught me was that if a coach wants you, she will call back later. Don't be nervous that she'll drop your name and move on to the next person without talking to you. Coaches usually have a lot of time and effort invested in recruiting you at this stage in the process. They want to see you on their team.

My final message to you in regards to speaking directly with a college coach is to try not to allow them to run you over. You might not have an answer to some of the questions a coach might ask you. For example, a coach might ask if you will commit to their team today. You might not be in a position to say "yes" or "no"; or maybe the question catches you so "off-guard" that you freeze up. Try not to say anything that you don't mean to say or be "giggly". If you can't answer a question, just tell them you aren't prepared to answer that question yet. It's best to say nothing and ask them to call back instead of saying something that you didn't want to say or making up a story. It's ok to be busy living your life and it's ok if you haven't made a decision yet! Honesty was always the best policy for me.

Here's a strategy that might help you. Have a friend call you and actually practice talking to her like she's a coach. Tell her what to say ahead of time so she's prepared. If you're really nervous and giggly on the phone, practicing with a friend just once or twice will help a lot for the real event!

Step 6 - Visiting Colleges:

Dad: $

If you are physically visiting an NCAA college, please visit the NCAA guidelines on line to be sure you are adhering to their rules and regulations surrounding visits. The NCAA web site is listed here for you. It is best to visit their web site to get the most up-to-date information including terminology, definitions, rules, guidelines, and calendars as some information does change from year-to-year. However, I will put some of the basic highlights here for you.

http://www.ncaa.org/

There are 2 basic visits that you can make to a prospective college.

The Official Visit
The Unofficial Visit

Below are the NCAA Div II definitions of the official and unofficial visit.

Official Visit is any visit to a college campus by you paid for by the college. You are allowed to make up to 5 official visits. The college may pay all or some of the following expenses:

- Your transportation to and from the college.
- Room and meals (three per day) while you are visiting the college.
- Reasonable entertainment expenses, including three complimentary admissions to a home athletics contest.

Before a college can invite you on an official visit, you will be required to provide the college with a copy of your high school transcript (Division I only) and SAT, ACT or PLAN score and register with the Eligibility Center.

Unofficial Visit is any visit by you to a college campus paid for by you. The only expenses you can receive from the college are three complimentary admissions to a home athletics contest.

You can make as many unofficial visits as you like and may take those visits at any time. The only time you cannot talk with a coach during an unofficial visit is during a dead period. (A dead period is when a college coach may <u>not</u> have any in-person contact with you or your parents; on or off campus at any time. However, the coach may write and telephone you or your parents during this time). This may be an area where you may want to retain the assistance of a consultant. Please refer to **www.mysoftballscholarship.com** for more information.

If a coach wants to extend an offer for an official visit, they will usually take care of the travel arrangements for you. They will want to control the time that you spend on campus so an itinerary will usually be created for you too. While visiting, you will get a good look at all aspects of the college campus including the softball program and facilities. Part of the visit also involves spending time with your prospective teammates by eating with them, going to some of their classes, and sleeping over at their dormitory. It's important to be on your toes during this time. You want to be relaxed and enjoy the experience, but at the same time, be careful what you say and do. The coach and or players may be testing you during this time. My advice is to just be yourself and make smart decisions while on campus.

Dad: $

Below is another e-mail that illustrates what some of the communication might look like when scheduling a college campus visit.

From: College Coach
To: Emily Poulton
Subject: College Visit

Hi Emily,

I spoke with your dad today about a potential visit to Study Hard College on October 15...we'd love to have you! I'd like to give you some additional information about it so that you can start planning your trip. Our fall break officially begins Friday, October 20 after classes, so I'm not exactly sure what the campus will be like that day. Everyone will probably be quite excited about the upcoming break!

Anyway, here's what I'm thinking: if you're able to get to campus around 9:00 AM or 10:00 AM, Coach Franks and I can meet with you and chat about Study Hard and the softball program. If we have time, we'll show you our athletic facilities. We'll then have a player come whisk you away and take you to an 11:00 AM class and then to lunch with the team. After that, Admissions holds a great information session at 1:30 PM, and then we'll try to get you a 2:30 PM Admissions interview. That will probably last 15 or 30 minutes, so after that, come back to the gym and Coach Franks and I will show you the athletic facilities (if we didn't have time earlier) and show you around campus. That should put us around 3:30 PM or 4:00 PM, and then you can head back to the airport.

If you're unable to get to campus that early in the morning, we can work out something else. I think the three most important things are meeting with us (which would also include the facilities tour), meeting the team, and having the admissions interview.

Let me know how all this sounds to you and what other information you might need. I'm looking forward to meeting you, so I'm confident that we'll be able to make something work.

Take care,

College Coach

College visits are such an exciting time for you and your parents. The next step after planning the trip is for you to actually take the trip! Let's hear from Emily about her college visits.

Emily:

Spring break of my junior year was a week that I'll never forget. I was escorted by one of my coaches on a trip to visit several colleges in New England, New York, and Pennsylvania. I was starting to get my list narrowed down to about 10 -15 colleges at this point. It was exciting to see the colleges and towns. I was even able to meet some of the coaches. When you go on an unofficial visit, it is usually relaxed so if the coaches are available, I found out that it is a really good idea to let them know you are there. They like to see the initiative that you are spending your own money just to come to see them. I noticed that it really helped to step up the communication with those coaches after I met them face-to-face.

Dad:

Emily didn't do any other college visits until the fall of her senior year in high school. By this time, she had her list down to 5 schools. Four of the colleges were DIII and one was DII. They were all a good fit academically and for her softball skill level. Three of the DIII schools were actively pursuing her and one was a school that Emily was pursuing. The DII college initiated the contact with Emily based on her e-mail with her skills video attached to it. Before the fall trip, we talked about the list and what order all of the colleges appeared. We thought we had a good idea of where she was going to go. Emily took the time to really think about the colleges and to prioritize them. At the time, I didn't realize just how important the campus visit was. Our list was turned upside down as soon as the airplane hit the ground. Emily will tell you that story.

Emily:

The first college that I saw on that trip was a really nice liberal arts DIII college. At the time, they were not #1 on my list. On our 30 minute drive from the airport to the campus, the coach called my cell phone. She was really excited and wanted to know if I could meet her on campus at the gym with my parents, even though it was about 9:00 PM after a long day on an airplane. We agreed and met her there. It was dark and we didn't know where we were going so of course my dad got lost on the way. But eventually he figured it out and got us there. When we got to the gym, the coach had 2 of the players from the team with her. She asked my mom and dad if it would be ok for me to stay in the dorm that night. I didn't even have time to react. Of course I said yes and off I went.

You know how sometimes when you meet someone, it just clicks? That's what happened to me on this trip. Everything just clicked. The girls on the team were really great. They took me out to dinner and we stayed up and talked until the early morning hours. It was like we were friends forever and knew each other for ten years. The next day they took me to breakfast and some classes. Then we all went to lunch while the assistant coach had lunch with my parents. We finished up the visit with a tour of the campus with the head and assistant coaches. It was really nice getting all of that personalized attention from the coaches. Only one other college treated me that way and it made all the difference in the world. It made me feel so comfortable. I left that visit thinking that this was definitely now my #1 college choice.

Dad: $

As a parent, I wanted to make sure that Emily did not get all wrapped up in the hype of the moment. She was really excited about this college. I have to admit, I was excited too. It is really nice to see your daughter treated so well by a college coach and the whole team. But we had 3 other college visits planned for this trip. So I did not want for her to make a quick decision before seeing the other colleges. After we talked about it, she agreed to try to keep an open mind for the rest of the trip.

The next college we visited was #1 on her list and my list. I say it that way because sometimes our lists were different. Big surprise, huh? ☺ It was a Div. III school with a very high standard of excellence in academics, but with a softball program that needed some help. During her unofficial visit with this college, everything went really well with our initial discussion with the coach in her office. She was very gracious and I could tell that she knew what she wanted. She said something in that meeting that I learned to be the "magic words" of recruiting. She said, "We want Emily." I learned that coaches don't say this unless they truly want to recruit your daughter. Emily was fortunate enough to hear these magic words from 3 colleges. I chalk that up to the fact that she did so much work with her e-mails and showcase events.

As is customary with a college visit, the SA then goes off to class, meals, and a sleep-over with some of the current members of the college team to experience the campus and to get to know the players. My wife and I were to meet Emily after lunch for a tour of the campus and a visit with the financial aid office. When we met, I immediately knew something was wrong by the look on Emily's face. As a parent, you know the look. She said that this was not what she wanted at all. She didn't feel welcomed by the team and she didn't like the overall feel of the college. We took the tour together and then walked over to the financial aid office. On the way, we talked. Emily quickly came to the conclusion that she did not want to attend this college. Normally, I would have asked her to finish out the experience. However, I could tell that the damage was done. Rather than force the issue we all decided to just go back to the coach and tell her that it wasn't working out. We did just that and left the campus. In a matter of a few short hours, her #1 school was off her list all together. It was with this experience that I learned how important it was for Emily to make the choices as to where she would attend college. Later on that day the coach called Emily to get more information. Emily shared with her how she was treated and how she felt. They decided to mutually leave the door open in the event that Emily changed her mind. From Emily's perspective, she told me that she was relieved that her list was getting shorter. The sun still came up the following morning. Life goes on…

Emily:

I was actually feeling relieved after this visit. I knew right away that this college was not going to be a good fit for me. I don't know how I knew, but I knew. When I met the girls on the team, I really knew it wasn't going to work out. I was treated like an outsider, not like someone who they wanted on their team. As expected, they took me to one of their classes. It was just so weird. After class, I was escorted to lunch by one of the girls. She didn't say one word to me. Just when I thought that I had been through the strangest experience ever, I traveled from Strangeville to Bizarretown and beyond! Once we arrived at the dining commons, we sat down at the lunch table to wait for the rest of the team. While sitting there, she just stared at the door and didn't talk to me. Finally, after what seemed like an eternity (in reality, it was probably about five minutes), everyone else showed up and lunch was served.

I was never so happy to see my parents when they met me to take the campus tour after lunch. I was psyched when they agreed not to force me to sleep overnight at this college. There was no way I was going here. What's strange is that it was ok with me. I thought it would be hard to reduce my college list down from five to the final one, but I knew right away that this one was not the right college for me. The decision was much easier than I thought it would be after visiting the campus.

> **Do not make a college choice unless you visit the campus. You may not know if you will like it unless you see the campus and meet the coach and team.**

Dad: 💲

At the time, while Emily was feeling "relieved" as she put it, I have to admit that I was a little nervous. In a matter of a few short hours during a college visit, this school was completely off her list. It was a lot to take in at the time. But we had faith that this process would lead us to a positive outcome. Besides, Emily had cast a large net in the beginning so she still had other schools on her list that were very much interested in her. And she was equally interested in them! We went on to visit 2 other colleges during that trip. As it turns out, the other 2 visits didn't impress Emily either. So now her list was down to 2 colleges. Something happened at one of the other schools that I think was important. Emily, take it away…

Emily: ✎

Now that I had a few college visits under my belt, I was better prepared for the rest of them. The more visits I did, the better I was getting at it. When we visited one of the other colleges that weekend, I learned to start asking more questions of the coach and try to be more observant in their office. What I heard and saw definitely let me know where I stood with this particular coach. Not directly, but if I really listened, this coach was telling me that she didn't really want me on her team. She told me she had 5 other catchers on her team already. I never heard of a team having 5 catchers before so this was a huge red flag for me. I know that sounds strange, but it happened. I knew right away that I was more interested in this college than they were in me.

One other thing jumped out at me that I'll never forget. She had a white board in her office with the names of all her top recruits written on it. My name wasn't on the list. When my parents and I were driving away from this one, they asked me what I thought. I told them what you just read above. My parents never saw the writing on the white board and we were all sitting in the same room! I felt pretty good about the fact that I noticed it. I wrote the coach an e-mail to thank her for taking the time to see us (as I always did) and never heard from her again.

Dad: $

College visits are a very exciting time for you and your parents, especially if it is an official visit. An official visit usually means that the college coach is very interested in you. In fact, you want to be prepared to receive an offer during the visit, assuming it goes well. That is exactly how it happened with Emily.

Thirteen days after Emily told her top choice that she was not attending their school; she flew across the country again to her first and only official visit. We took a red eye flight to meet the coach first thing in the morning after our arrival. Emily got some sleep on the plane but I think my nerves got the better of me. I enjoyed several movies on the plane but I got about one half hour of sleep. As expected, Emily's day was well planned with no time to spare. The coach picked us up at the airport. We got a great tour of the campus, ate at the dining commons, met the team, and even met some other recruits. At the end of the day, Emily got to practice with the team. After practice, I went to a hotel for some sleep and Emily went to the dormitory with her team mates. Despite being nervous about whether she would be invited to attend this college, I was so tired that I found sleep very easily that night. The next day the coach invited us to breakfast before she dropped us off at the airport. It was then that we heard those magic words again. "We want Emily." Once I heard it, I knew everything was going to be ok. The coach informed us about the rest of the process, her thoughts on the financial package, and time frames involved. The coach had a firm grasp on the process so it took a lot of the unknown out of the equation for Emily and me. The college was able to get everything to us so early that Emily signed early decision (see more on early decision in the next section). As it turns out, Emily signed her NLI just 26 short days after she walked away from what we thought was her #1 school choice mentioned earlier. The school she committed to and is attending was just a much better fit for her, scholastically and athletically.

Emily:

As good as my first unofficial visit was that I described earlier, this official visit was just as good, if not better. As I look back on it now, what set the two top colleges apart from the rest was how the coaches and team treated me; especially the coach. I can tell you that if a coach doesn't take the time to show you around the campus and spend a good chunk of time with you while you are at their college, they probably don't really want you. Maybe they wouldn't mind having you but you might not be high on their list. This coach was really great! She basically set aside the whole day just for me. She told me how she's building the softball program and how she saw me fitting into the puzzle. She painted the picture so I could easily see how I would fit into her plan. She told me that she needed a catcher that she could count on to be a leader on the field. She said she usually doesn't go by what she sees on a video, but in my case, she saw the leadership that she felt was needed on her squad.

> **Side Note:** I didn't set out to create a video that showcased my leadership skills, but that's what came across on it. So to repeat what we've been saying all along, be sure to send out your video to as many coaches as possible (cast a large net). You don't know where you'll be a good fit and you definitely don't know what a coach might be looking for to round out the team.

Emily:

Getting back to my story, the coach showed my dad and me around town, campus and the softball facilities. She was totally professional in everything she did. I could also see the pride that she had for her college, her team, and the softball program that she was building. She was excited which got me excited too. I think excitement is infectious in a good way! That was important to me. I try to give 150% with everything I do so when the coach showed me that she treats her team the same way, I knew it was a great fit for me. I would encourage you to look for qualities in your college coach that are important to you when you visit with them. If your goals are the same as theirs, chances are good that the softball program will be a good fit for you.

I'll end my story with this one last item. There is one other thing that influenced my decision making process. It's not really something that I can put my finger on. Much of what influenced my decision was the feeling in my gut. I heard other softball players tell me about this when I was in high school. I heard them say that I would know when it was the right school. They said that I would just know it in my heart or the pit of my stomach. They were right! I knew right away. I knew when the school <u>wasn't</u> a good fit. And I also knew when it <u>was</u> a good fit. Try to keep an open mind throughout the process, but listen to how you feel inside. Leave all doors open and as you heard my dad say over and over again; cast a large net so you have lots of opportunities! This process works. Now I'm living the dream!

Step 7 – The Application

Dad: $

Early Decision vs. Early Action vs. Single Choice Early Action vs. Regular Acceptance Period

If you find a college that you know is the absolute right choice for you, then you should consider applying early. The process that you have gone through in this book will often put you in position to take advantage of this great opportunity. While your peers are still looking for a college, you will be enjoying the rest of your senior year in high school with much of the stress off of your shoulders. Early decision and early action plans allow you to apply early (usually in November) and get an early admissions decision from the college. This puts you in front of all the other students that will apply in the normal spring notification period. This way, you may know as early as November whether you have been accepted at your first-choice college! This is true especially in the sports arena as the early signing date for most sports is in mid-November. Check the NLI web site (next chapter) for specific dates for early signing. Also check with your prospective college for their deadlines as they may differ.

Emily and I were both told that most applicants who apply early may have a better chance of acceptance and better financial aid packages than they would through the regular admissions process. This is due to the fact that the college has not spent all of their financial aid dollars yet. So in a way, you get to be first in line for all the goodies! These plans are also good for colleges, because they get students who really want to go to the school to commit early in the process. It takes the SA out of the shopping mode.

Early Decision:
You need to know a few specifics about early decision. Early decision is binding. The definition of binding is that it imposes an obligation or duty to you. In other words, you agree to attend the college if it accepts you and offers a mutually acceptable financial aid package to you. It is important to know that you can apply to only one college for early decision. However, you can also apply to other colleges through the regular admissions process. If you are accepted by your first-choice college early, you must withdraw all of your other applications. To cement the deal, the college that accepts you early will most likely request a nominal nonrefundable deposit from you.

Early Action:
Another option for you is something called early action. Early action is similar to early decision but it is not binding. If you get accepted with early action, you can choose to commit to the college immediately, or you can wait until spring if you like. You have the option to apply early action to other colleges as well. When you are applying with early action, you usually have until late spring to let the college know your decision. With early action, you risk nothing with this option. Due to the fact that it is not binding, it is a good way to either eliminate or seriously consider this school.

Single Choice Early Action
A new option offered by some schools is called single choice early action. This works the same way as other early action plans, but you cannot apply early (either early action or early decision) to any other school. You can still apply to other schools but you are not required to give a final answer of acceptance until their regular decision deadline. So the benefits here are that you get to "play the field" for a bit longer; a good choice if you are not sure about where you want to go.

Regular Acceptance Period
Applications for most colleges are due between the months of November through January for the regular acceptance period. Time frames vary by state and college or university so it is best to check with each individual school's web site for specifics on their application

due date. As a general rule, colleges are required to notify you by April 1st if you are accepted or not. You will then have until May 1st to accept or decline their offer of acceptance.

Just keep in mind that the longer you take to decide, the lower your chances are of getting into your first choice college with a scholarship. If you have done all of the work in this book, you will usually be in good shape to make an early decision if that option is presented to you.

Step 8 - The Offer - National Letter of Intent (NLI)

Dad: $

If you are looking at an NCAA DI and DII college, then this is the prize that you are working to achieve! It's the document that actually puts the commitment from the college into writing. Assuming you did well on your visit to the college and the coach wants to invite you to play there, this is the document that seals the deal! The National Letter of Intent (NLI) is a voluntary program administered by the Eligibility Center. By signing an NLI, you agree to attend the college for one academic year. In exchange, that college must provide athletic financial aid for one academic year. Restrictions are contained in the NLI itself. Read them carefully as these restrictions may affect your eligibility.

Once the NLI is signed, the SA is no longer subject to further recruiting contacts and calls. SA's are assured of an athletics scholarship for one full academic year. Remember, your NLI is a commitment to the college, not the particular coach or team. It is a good idea to advise any coaches that you were speaking to up to this point that you have signed your NLI. It lets them know that you have committed to a college so they can direct their efforts towards other recruits. Plus I feel that it's just the right thing to do. These two little paragraphs don't look like much, but the NLI is the actual form that you having been working all these years to receive. To quote one of Emily's and my favorite movies, *Willy Wonka & the Chocolate Factory*, **"I've got the golden ticket!"**

Below are links for more information:

www.mysoftballscholarship.com

http://www.ncaa.org/wps/wcm/connect/nli/NLI/Home/

www.national-letter.org

Financial Aid Information

Dad: $

In the NCAA, athletic scholarships are only awarded by Division I and II colleges. Division III schools do not award financial aid based on an athlete's ability. The good news is that you may be eligible to receive academic scholarships or need-based financial aid. It is important to understand several points about athletic scholarships.

• **Athletic scholarships in Divisions I and II are given initially for up to one year.** They may be renewed annually for a maximum of five years within a six-year period of continuous college attendance if you fulfill NCAA requirements. But please keep in mind that your athletics aid can be cancelled or reduced at the end of one year. I put this here to dispel things that you might hear on the street and to properly arm you with information. We have all heard the story about the player that got a 4 year full ride to XYZ University. While it is true that a college can offer a full ride and a player can accept it, the truth of the matter is that it's a year-to-year renewable commitment.

- **Athletics scholarships can be renewed, reduced, increased or canceled from year to year for almost any reason.** If your scholarship is going to be reduced or cancelled at any time, your college or university must first provide you with an opportunity to appeal that decision. This point just elaborates on what I said in the previous bullet point.

- **Athletics scholarships are awarded in a variety of amounts.** These range from full scholarships (including tuition, fees, room, board, and books) to very small scholarships that, for example, provide only required course-related books. The scholarship is usually negotiable. Therefore, when you start to hear the college coach talk about the scholarship offer, pay close attention and be sure to ask questions so you understand exactly what all the details are surrounding the offer. If you do not understand something about the offer, ask questions for clarification.

- **Once you receive a scholarship, you want to be careful about accepting other funds from other sources.** For example, your college tuition, room and board may cost $25,000 per year. The college has offered to pay $15,000 per year for an athletic scholarship leaving you with $10,000 per year. You may think its ok to apply for other academic scholarships to cover the remaining $10,000. You may be ok if you do receive other funds from other sources but you also might be jeopardizing your athletic scholarship. Therefore, you must report all scholarships you receive to your college financial aid office before you accept them. Do not accept the funds and then tell the college later. A mistake here could have tragic consequences. The total amount of financial aid a student athlete can receive and the total amount of athletics aid a team can award may be limited based on many factors that you do not know about. These limits can affect whether a student-athlete may accept additional financial aid from other sources. Ask the financial aid officials at your college about other financial aid you may be eligible to receive. Also, ask them about the impact of additional aid and limits to your athletic scholarship. This will help to prevent you from possibly losing a scholarship offer. As I am sure you know, an athletic scholarship is a great benefit to most families, but you should have a plan to pay for those college costs not covered by a scholarship (i.e., travel between home and school and miscellaneous expenses).

Step 9 - What Happens After I Sign?

Dad: $

After you sign your NLI or verbally agree to attend the college of you choice, there are still a few things you need to stay focused on.

- What ever agreement you made with your college, make sure you honor your side of the agreement. For example:
  - o There may be minimum grade standards that you need to maintain to continue to be eligible.
  - o They may request that you maintain some level of fitness between the time you sign and the start of your college career. For example, they may require that members of their team can run 1 mile in a certain period of time or complete 25 sit-ups in a certain period of time, etc…
  - o Your college coach may want you to continue to keep them updated with your successes and/or concerns.

- Make sure you understand your college eligibility requirements. In other words, don't do anything that would jeopardize your eligibility with your college or college coach. If in doubt, do not do or say it. For example, I knew a person that had a "full ride" to a nice college for about $30,000 per year (that's $120,000 for 4 years). While still in high school, this student said something in confidence to one of their new college teammates. The teammate repeated it to the coach. I don't know exactly what it was, but the coach immediately called the SA and withdrew the scholarship offer. Luckily, this SA was gifted and quickly got a "full ride" at another school. But only after many stressful weeks of having to restart the process after they thought they were finished. I can't even imagine the anxiety...

  After you get your scholarship, do not think that now is the time to change your habits that you have been living under throughout this process. Your college and coach expect you to maintain the standards of excellence that they saw while they were recruiting you.

- If your college coach gives you a summer workout packet to work on, work on it faithfully and expect to be tested on your physical ability when you show up to your first team practice. Be warned… incoming first year college students that show up out of shape will definitely receive some unwanted attention from coaches and teammates.

- Continue to play your sport at the amateur level. I am sure by now that you realize that you will continue to work on your skill set before and after you enter your college career. Keep working on it. Now is a good time to set some new goals. Do you want to strive to be a Collegiate All American? Perhaps you have some classroom goals that you want to set. What do you want your GPA to be when you graduate? You know the drill. Write your new S.M.A.R.T goals here:

My new S.M.A.R.T. goals are: Date: _____

_____
_____
_____
_____
_____
_____
_____
_____
_____
_____
_____

4

Other Stuff Just For Grins And Giggles

Dad: $

Picking a Club/Travel Team:
Choosing a team to play with outside of high school is a very personal decision. I would like to hit on two things to consider: Play Time & Team Coach and Public Relations (PR) Coach.

Play Time with your Club/Travel Team:
In regards to play time, remember this when looking at a team. Besides looking at the relationship with the coach, the team's record, the relationship with the other players on the team, I offer the following thought starter: Is play time as important as the level of play with this team? What I mean here is this: Is it important to be on the "best team"? Is your goal to be on the team with the best record and all the best players; or is it important to be on the team where you can get the most playing time? It is an important part of the SA's decision. It is nice to decide to "play up" at a higher level than where you are now, but one must weigh that decision against how much play time they get. You will probably laugh when you read this but most college coaches want to see you actually playing on the field of play! Emily was on a great team when she was 13 -15 years old. The team was stacked! They placed 7th at

ASA Nationals. It was a great thrill but Emily did not see much play time. The talent pool on that team certainly helped develop Emily's skill level. I believe you play up or play down depending on who is playing around you on your team. But in order to really improve your skills, you have to be tested in live game situations. It wasn't until after she left that team and started playing in almost every game on a different team that she realized how well she played. I also saw a great deal of maturity and confidence growth in Emily during that time.

> The moral of the story here is that you may not have to play on the best team in the league to get a softball college scholarship.
> You just have to play *your* best!

Team Coach and Public Relations (PR) Coach:
More and more teams are moving toward this concept. In one form or another, what this means is that the team has a coach or coaches that maintain the team on the field and at practice while employing a totally different coach whose job is to assist the SA with the college recruiting process. The PR Coach will wear many hats including helping the SA with paperwork, watch grades, watch SAT dates, and even promote the SA to college coaches while attending showcase events. This can be a very beneficial part of a team in assisting you with your goals. When choosing a team, ask the coach if they have one.

Professional Athlete vs. Professional Student
I do not want to dwell on this too much or burst anyone's bubble that may have an actual shot at a professional athletic career. I also do not want to recommend in any way that you shouldn't strive for a professional career in your sport. This paragraph is here for the rest of us who will not make it that far. My comment here is just to keep things in perspective. While you may be a standout athlete right now, you will quickly see that you are entering into a smaller pool of gifted athletes, just like yourself. Whether you are the greatest athlete or lowest level player on your team, make sure you maintain your grades and your studies. I pose three simple reasons for this:

- The first reason is that your coach may have a minimum GPA set for all members of the team. If your GPA is below the team average, you do not want to be the person on your coach's radar screen that is pulling the team's GPA average down. Many college coaches take a great deal of pride in their team's GPA. Some may even depend on it for their pay rate and job security. After all, their employer is an academic institution or a place for learning. Ask your college coach about this and you will see what I mean.

- Your scholarship may be contingent upon you maintaining a certain GPA. In other words, in order for the scholarship to continue, you have to maintain your grades at a certain level in order to continue to receive it. If your grades drop below a certain level, you may lose the scholarship money.

- The last item is for you to remember that you will be a professional "<u>something</u>" when you graduate from college. You might be a professional teacher, a professional attorney, a professional engineer, a professional coach, or a professional physical therapist. You get the idea. Whatever it is that you end up doing with your life; that will be your profession. Even if you do make it to be a professional athlete, your body does not hold up forever. At some point you will leave this high level sports arena as an athlete. So you will want to have a back up plan or a plan "B" as I call it. Actually, this plan should be your plan "A" and everything else should be your plan "B". Enjoy your time as an athlete. Strive to be your best at all times. Also strive to be your best in the classroom too so you have a career to earn a living after your days on the field are behind you. As my three daughters say, "Sorry to be a Debbie Downer"! It is a reality check and needs to be said.

Peer Reaction:
After you have reached your goal and are signed at a college you have no idea how others are going to react. Some will treat you differently (good and bad). Be proud but not boastful. Just be aware that you have accomplished something that most others only dream of. You have elevated yourself to play at the collegiate level of your sport! Congratulations! You are living the dream!

High School and Club/Travel Coaches as a Resource:
The final topic I want to touch on is using your High School and Club/Travel Coaches as a resource. Let them know what your desires are. Talk to them. Share information with them. Do not have your parents do this for you. Talk with them yourself. In most cases, you will find that they really care about you and truly want to help you to be successful. Many of these coaches are in this for the love of the game, or because they have a child in

the sport, or they just have a passion to help others succeed. So let them in. Say, "Thanks Coach" when it's all over…

For more information on how your coach can participate with you in this process, please refer to the Coach's Corner on www.mysoftballscholarship.com.

Emily's Closing Comments :

Well, there you have it. Follow these steps and you'll have a good chance at earning a college softball scholarship. As with anything in life, there are no guarantees, but at least you'll be working towards your goal. I want to close the book by just saying a few words to the softball players reading this book, and then to their parents.

The first and by far most important message that I want to share is for you to never let others bring you down, tell you that you're not good enough, or say that you'll never play in college or past high school. Stay as far away from people who talk like that as you can.

No matter what coach you play for or what team you're on, make sure you are happy. Once you are not happy with your situation, you will probably stop playing. Sounds simple but I mention it so you can keep your eye on it.

Keep in contact with past coaches and don't burn bridges. I put these together because I witnessed many girls who left a team and totally trashed it on their way out the door. Take the high road and try to avoid the negativity that sometimes goes along with switching teams. Those past coaches may be a great resource for you later on in the process. Plus you never know when you might decide to go back to the team at a later date. Funny things happen in the game of softball!

The last item I want to say to you, the softball player, is about the process itself. Try to make it a "clean" process. What I mean here is for you to try to make good decisions so you can enjoy all that your high school and the game of softball have to offer. Things like skipping class, goofing off, or maybe even something more serious may be tempting when your friends are doing it, but somehow, your coach always finds out about stuff like that. Why let a bad decision you made off the field affect what you do on the field? It's just not worth the gamble. Keep it clean…

I also wanted to take the opportunity to speak to the parents who are reading this. Most of my comments in the book have been to your daughters, so I didn't want to miss this opportunity. Take a quick look back at the beginning of the book where I described how it all started for me. I really just want to bring out two points.

The first is a request to try not to underestimate the value of the experience of your child while they are early in their sport experience. What I mean is, if it were not for me making that first all-star team when I was 12 years old, I don't think that I would have pursued my softball career the way I did. It was the springboard that launched me into everything else I did because it got me excited about softball.

The second is that it got me excited about the friends I've made through softball and the positive way that it can affect me and my friend's lives. My dad still has the picture of my 2004 all-star team on his desk in his home office so I look at it all the time. This picture was taken right after we won the Southern California Championship game. I guess we weren't really supposed to win but what did we know? We were proudly wearing our medals, holding up the championship banner, and we had our arms around each other. It was a memory that I'll never forget. There were only 12 girls on that team. As of this writing; of those twelve girls, seven are now, or will be playing college softball at either DI, DII, DIII, NAIA, or at a Junior College. Six of those 7 are in a DI, DII, or DIII NCAA program, most with some kind of scholarship. Coming from a 12U Little League team, to see 58% of your team continue on to college softball is something that I'm very proud of!

Those early years laid the ground work. We were only 12 years old but it all started right there. Where will your daughter's journey start?

---

www.mysoftballscholarship.com

For more information, to contact the authors, and for additional services; please visit our web site!

Appendix A

College List:

Reach Schools: **Date:** _____

1. College Name: _____ Web Site: _____

   NCAA ___ DI ___ DII ___ DIII   ___ NAIA   ___JC

   Coach Name: _____ E-mail: _____

   Coach Telephone Number: _____

2. College Name: _____ Web Site: _____

   NCAA ___ DI ___ DII ___ DIII   ___ NAIA   ___JC

   Coach Name: _____ E-mail: _____

   Coach Telephone Number: _____

3. College Name: _____ Web Site: _____

    NCAA ___ DI ___ DII ___ DIII   ___ NAIA   ___JC

    Coach Name: _____ E-mail: _____

    Coach Telephone Number: _____

4. College Name: _____ Web Site: _____

    NCAA ___ DI ___ DII ___ DIII   ___ NAIA   ___JC

    Coach Name: _____ E-mail: _____

    Coach Telephone Number: _____

5. College Name: _____ Web Site: _____

    NCAA ___ DI ___ DII ___ DIII   ___ NAIA   ___JC

    Coach Name: _____ E-mail: _____

    Coach Telephone Number: _____

6. College Name: _____ Web Site: _____

    NCAA ___ DI ___ DII ___ DIII   ___ NAIA   ___JC

    Coach Name: _____ E-mail: _____

    Coach Telephone Number: _____

7. College Name: _____ Web Site: _____

    NCAA ___ DI ___ DII ___ DIII   ___ NAIA   ___JC

    Coach Name: _____ E-mail: _____

    Coach Telephone Number: _____

8. College Name: _____ Web Site: _____

   NCAA ___ DI ___ DII ___ DIII   ___ NAIA   ___JC

   Coach Name: _____ E-mail: _____

   Coach Telephone Number: _____

9. College Name: _____ Web Site: _____

   NCAA ___ DI ___ DII ___ DIII   ___ NAIA   ___JC

   Coach Name: _____ E-mail: _____

   Coach Telephone Number: _____

10. College Name: _____ Web Site: _____

   NCAA ___ DI ___ DII ___ DIII   ___ NAIA   ___JC

   Coach Name: _____ E-mail: _____

   Coach Telephone Number: _____

11. College Name: _____ Web Site: _____

   NCAA ___ DI ___ DII ___ DIII   ___ NAIA   ___JC

   Coach Name: _____ E-mail: _____

   Coach Telephone Number: _____

12. College Name: _____ Web Site: _____

   NCAA ___ DI ___ DII ___ DIII   ___ NAIA   ___JC

   Coach Name: _____ E-mail: _____

   Coach Telephone Number: _____

13. College Name: _____ Web Site: _____

    NCAA ___ DI ___ DII ___ DIII   ___ NAIA   ___JC

    Coach Name: _____ E-mail: _____

    Coach Telephone Number: _____

14. College Name: _____ Web Site: _____

    NCAA ___ DI ___ DII ___ DIII   ___ NAIA   ___JC

    Coach Name: _____ E-mail: _____

    Coach Telephone Number: _____

15. College Name: _____ Web Site: _____

    NCAA ___ DI ___ DII ___ DIII   ___ NAIA   ___JC

    Coach Name: _____ E-mail: _____

    Coach Telephone Number: _____

16. College Name: _____ Web Site: _____

    NCAA ___ DI ___ DII ___ DIII   ___ NAIA   ___JC

    Coach Name: _____ E-mail: _____

    Coach Telephone Number: _____

17. College Name: _____ Web Site: _____

    NCAA ___ DI ___ DII ___ DIII   ___ NAIA   ___JC

    Coach Name: _____ E-mail: _____

    Coach Telephone Number: _____

18. College Name: _____ Web Site: _____

    NCAA ___ DI ___ DII ___ DIII   ___ NAIA   ___JC

    Coach Name: _____ E-mail: _____

    Coach Telephone Number: _____

19. College Name: _____ Web Site: _____

    NCAA ___ DI ___ DII ___ DIII   ___ NAIA   ___JC

    Coach Name: _____ E-mail: _____

    Coach Telephone Number: _____

20. College Name: _____ Web Site: _____

    NCAA ___ DI ___ DII ___ DIII   ___ NAIA   ___JC

    Coach Name: _____ E-mail: _____

    Coach Telephone Number: _____

21. College Name: _____ Web Site: _____

    NCAA ___ DI ___ DII ___ DIII   ___ NAIA   ___JC

    Coach Name: _____ E-mail: _____

    Coach Telephone Number: _____

22. College Name: _____ Web Site: _____

    NCAA ___ DI ___ DII ___ DIII   ___ NAIA   ___JC

    Coach Name: _____ E-mail: _____

    Coach Telephone Number: _____

23. College Name: _____ Web Site: _____

    NCAA ___ DI ___ DII ___ DIII   ___ NAIA   ___JC

    Coach Name: _____ E-mail: _____

    Coach Telephone Number: _____

24. College Name: _____ Web Site: _____

    NCAA ___ DI ___ DII ___ DIII   ___ NAIA   ___JC

    Coach Name: _____ E-mail: _____

    Coach Telephone Number: _____

25. College Name: _____ Web Site: _____

    NCAA ___ DI ___ DII ___ DIII   ___ NAIA   ___JC

    Coach Name: _____ E-mail: _____

    Coach Telephone Number: _____

26. College Name: _____ Web Site: _____

    NCAA ___ DI ___ DII ___ DIII   ___ NAIA   ___JC

    Coach Name: _____ E-mail: _____

    Coach Telephone Number: _____

27. College Name: _____ Web Site: _____

    NCAA ___ DI ___ DII ___ DIII   ___ NAIA   ___JC

    Coach Name: _____ E-mail: _____

    Coach Telephone Number: _____

28. College Name: _____ Web Site: _____

   NCAA ___ DI ___ DII ___ DIII   ___ NAIA   ___JC

   Coach Name: _____ E-mail: _____

   Coach Telephone Number: _____

29. College Name: _____ Web Site: _____

   NCAA ___ DI ___ DII ___ DIII   ___ NAIA   ___JC

   Coach Name: _____ E-mail: _____

   Coach Telephone Number: _____

30. College Name: _____ Web Site: _____

   NCAA ___ DI ___ DII ___ DIII   ___ NAIA   ___JC

   Coach Name: _____ E-mail: _____

   Coach Telephone Number: _____

31. College Name: _____ Web Site: _____

   NCAA ___ DI ___ DII ___ DIII   ___ NAIA   ___JC

   Coach Name: _____ E-mail: _____

   Coach Telephone Number: _____

32. College Name: _____ Web Site: _____

   NCAA ___ DI ___ DII ___ DIII   ___ NAIA   ___JC

   Coach Name: _____ E-mail: _____

   Coach Telephone Number: _____

33. College Name: _____ Web Site: _____

    NCAA ___ DI ___ DII ___ DIII   ___ NAIA   ___JC

    Coach Name: _____ E-mail: _____

    Coach Telephone Number: _____

34. College Name: _____ Web Site: _____

    NCAA ___ DI ___ DII ___ DIII   ___ NAIA   ___JC

    Coach Name: _____ E-mail: _____

    Coach Telephone Number: _____

35. College Name: _____ Web Site: _____

    NCAA ___ DI ___ DII ___ DIII   ___ NAIA   ___JC

    Coach Name: _____ E-mail: _____

    Coach Telephone Number: _____

36. College Name: _____ Web Site: _____

    NCAA ___ DI ___ DII ___ DIII   ___ NAIA   ___JC

    Coach Name: _____ E-mail: _____

    Coach Telephone Number: _____

37. College Name: _____ Web Site: _____

    NCAA ___ DI ___ DII ___ DIII   ___ NAIA   ___JC

    Coach Name: _____ E-mail: _____

    Coach Telephone Number: _____

38. College Name: _____ Web Site: _____

    NCAA ___ DI ___ DII ___ DIII   ___ NAIA   ___JC

    Coach Name: _____ E-mail: _____

    Coach Telephone Number: _____

39. College Name: _____ Web Site: _____

    NCAA ___ DI ___ DII ___ DIII   ___ NAIA   ___JC

    Coach Name: _____ E-mail: _____

    Coach Telephone Number: _____

Attainable Schools: **Date:** _____

1. College Name: _____ Web Site: _____

   NCAA ___ DI ___ DII ___ DIII   ___ NAIA   ___JC

   Coach Name: _____ E-mail: _____

   Coach Telephone Number: _____

2. College Name: _____ Web Site: _____

   NCAA ___ DI ___ DII ___ DIII   ___ NAIA   ___JC

   Coach Name: _____ E-mail: _____

   Coach Telephone Number: _____

3. College Name: _____ Web Site: _____

   NCAA ___ DI ___ DII ___ DIII   ___ NAIA   ___JC

   Coach Name: _____ E-mail: _____

   Coach Telephone Number: _____

4. College Name: _____ Web Site: _____

   NCAA ___ DI ___ DII ___ DIII   ___ NAIA   ___JC

   Coach Name: _____ E-mail: _____

   Coach Telephone Number: _____

5. College Name: _____ Web Site: _____

   NCAA ___ DI ___ DII ___ DIII   ___ NAIA   ___JC

   Coach Name: _____ E-mail: _____

   Coach Telephone Number: _____

6. College Name: _____ Web Site: _____

   NCAA ___ DI ___ DII ___ DIII   ___ NAIA   ___JC

   Coach Name: _____ E-mail: _____

   Coach Telephone Number: _____

7. College Name: _____ Web Site: _____

   NCAA ___ DI ___ DII ___ DIII   ___ NAIA   ___JC

   Coach Name: _____ E-mail: _____

   Coach Telephone Number: _____

8. College Name: _____ Web Site: _____

   NCAA ___ DI ___ DII ___ DIII   ___ NAIA   ___JC

   Coach Name: _____ E-mail: _____

   Coach Telephone Number: _____

9. College Name: _____ Web Site: _____

   NCAA ___ DI ___ DII ___ DIII   ___ NAIA   ___JC

   Coach Name: _____ E-mail: _____

   Coach Telephone Number: _____

10. College Name: _____ Web Site: _____

    NCAA ___ DI ___ DII ___ DIII   ___ NAIA   ___JC

    Coach Name: _____ E-mail: _____

    Coach Telephone Number: _____

11. College Name: _____ Web Site: _____

    NCAA ___ DI ___ DII ___ DIII   ___ NAIA   ___JC

    Coach Name: _____ E-mail: _____

    Coach Telephone Number: _____

12. College Name: _____ Web Site: _____

    NCAA ___ DI ___ DII ___ DIII   ___ NAIA   ___JC

    Coach Name: _____ E-mail: _____

    Coach Telephone Number: _____

13. College Name: _____ Web Site: _____

    NCAA ___ DI ___ DII ___ DIII   ___ NAIA   ___JC

    Coach Name: _____ E-mail: _____

    Coach Telephone Number: _____

14. College Name: _____ Web Site: _____

    NCAA ___ DI ___ DII ___ DIII   ___ NAIA   ___JC

    Coach Name: _____ E-mail: _____

    Coach Telephone Number: _____

15. College Name: _____ Web Site: _____

    NCAA ___ DI ___ DII ___ DIII   ___ NAIA   ___JC

    Coach Name: _____ E-mail: _____

    Coach Telephone Number: _____

16. College Name: _____ Web Site: _____

    NCAA ___ DI ___ DII ___ DIII   ___ NAIA   ___JC

    Coach Name: _____ E-mail: _____

    Coach Telephone Number: _____

17. College Name: _____ Web Site: _____

    NCAA ___ DI ___ DII ___ DIII   ___ NAIA   ___JC

    Coach Name: _____ E-mail: _____

    Coach Telephone Number: _____

18. College Name: _____ Web Site: _____

    NCAA ___ DI ___ DII ___ DIII   ___ NAIA   ___JC

    Coach Name: _____ E-mail: _____

    Coach Telephone Number: _____

19. College Name: _____ Web Site: _____

    NCAA ___ DI ___ DII ___ DIII   ___ NAIA   ___JC

    Coach Name: _____ E-mail: _____

    Coach Telephone Number: _____

20. College Name: _____ Web Site: _____

    NCAA ___ DI ___ DII ___ DIII   ___ NAIA   ___JC

    Coach Name: _____ E-mail: _____

    Coach Telephone Number: _____

21. College Name: _____ Web Site: _____

    NCAA ___ DI ___ DII ___ DIII   ___ NAIA   ___JC

    Coach Name: _____ E-mail: _____

    Coach Telephone Number: _____

22. College Name: _____ Web Site: _____

    NCAA ___ DI ___ DII ___ DIII   ___ NAIA   ___JC

    Coach Name: _____ E-mail: _____

    Coach Telephone Number: _____

23. College Name: _____ Web Site: _____

    NCAA ___ DI ___ DII ___ DIII   ___ NAIA   ___JC

    Coach Name: _____ E-mail: _____

    Coach Telephone Number: _____

24. College Name: _____ Web Site: _____

    NCAA ___ DI ___ DII ___ DIII   ___ NAIA   ___JC

    Coach Name: _____ E-mail: _____

    Coach Telephone Number: _____

25. College Name: _____ Web Site: _____

    NCAA ___ DI ___ DII ___ DIII   ___ NAIA   ___JC

    Coach Name: _____ E-mail: _____

    Coach Telephone Number: _____

26. College Name: _____ Web Site: _____

    NCAA ___ DI ___ DII ___ DIII   ___ NAIA   ___JC

    Coach Name: _____ E-mail: _____

    Coach Telephone Number: _____

27. College Name: _____ Web Site: _____

    NCAA ___ DI ___ DII ___ DIII   ___ NAIA   ___JC

    Coach Name: _____ E-mail: _____

    Coach Telephone Number: _____

28. College Name: _____ Web Site: _____

    NCAA ___ DI ___ DII ___ DIII   ___ NAIA   ___JC

    Coach Name: _____ E-mail: _____

    Coach Telephone Number: _____

29. College Name: _____ Web Site: _____

    NCAA ___ DI ___ DII ___ DIII   ___ NAIA   ___JC

    Coach Name: _____ E-mail: _____

    Coach Telephone Number: _____

30. College Name: _____ Web Site: _____

    NCAA ___ DI ___ DII ___ DIII   ___ NAIA   ___JC

    Coach Name: _____ E-mail: _____

    Coach Telephone Number: _____

31. College Name: _____ Web Site: _____

    NCAA ___ DI ___ DII ___ DIII   ___ NAIA   ___JC

    Coach Name: _____ E-mail: _____

    Coach Telephone Number: _____

32. College Name: _____ Web Site: _____

    NCAA ___ DI ___ DII ___ DIII   ___ NAIA   ___JC

    Coach Name: _____ E-mail: _____

    Coach Telephone Number: _____

33. College Name: _____ Web Site: _____

    NCAA ___ DI ___ DII ___ DIII   ___ NAIA   ___JC

    Coach Name: _____ E-mail: _____

    Coach Telephone Number: _____

34. College Name: _____ Web Site: _____

    NCAA ___ DI ___ DII ___ DIII   ___ NAIA   ___JC

    Coach Name: _____ E-mail: _____

    Coach Telephone Number: _____

35. College Name: _____ Web Site: _____

    NCAA ___ DI ___ DII ___ DIII   ___ NAIA   ___JC

    Coach Name: _____ E-mail: _____

    Coach Telephone Number: _____

36. College Name: _____ Web Site: _____

    NCAA ___ DI ___ DII ___ DIII   ___ NAIA   ___JC

    Coach Name: _____ E-mail: _____

    Coach Telephone Number: _____

37. College Name: _____ Web Site: _____

    NCAA ___ DI ___ DII ___ DIII   ___ NAIA   ___JC

    Coach Name: _____ E-mail: _____

    Coach Telephone Number: _____

38. College Name: _____ Web Site: _____

    NCAA ___ DI ___ DII ___ DIII   ___ NAIA   ___JC

    Coach Name: _____ E-mail: _____

    Coach Telephone Number: _____

39. College Name: _____ Web Site: _____

    NCAA ___ DI ___ DII ___ DIII   ___ NAIA   ___JC

    Coach Name: _____ E-mail: _____

    Coach Telephone Number: _____

40. College Name: _____ Web Site: _____

    NCAA ___ DI ___ DII ___ DIII   ___ NAIA   ___JC

    Coach Name: _____ E-mail: _____

    Coach Telephone Number: _____

41. College Name: _____ Web Site: _____

    NCAA ___ DI ___ DII ___ DIII   ___ NAIA   ___JC

    Coach Name: _____ E-mail: _____

    Coach Telephone Number: _____

42. College Name: _____ Web Site: _____

    NCAA ___ DI ___ DII ___ DIII   ___ NAIA   ___JC

    Coach Name: _____ E-mail: _____

    Coach Telephone Number: _____

43. College Name: _____ Web Site: _____

    NCAA ___ DI ___ DII ___ DIII   ___ NAIA   ___JC

    Coach Name: _____ E-mail: _____

    Coach Telephone Number: _____

44. College Name: _____ Web Site: _____

    NCAA ___ DI ___ DII ___ DIII   ___ NAIA   ___JC

    Coach Name: _____ E-mail: _____

    Coach Telephone Number: _____

45. College Name: _____ Web Site: _____

    NCAA ___ DI ___ DII ___ DIII   ___ NAIA   ___JC

    Coach Name: _____ E-mail: _____

    Coach Telephone Number: _____

46. College Name: _____ Web Site: _____

    NCAA ___ DI ___ DII ___ DIII   ___ NAIA   ___JC

    Coach Name: _____ E-mail: _____

    Coach Telephone Number: _____

47. College Name: _____ Web Site: _____

    NCAA ___ DI ___ DII ___ DIII   ___ NAIA   ___JC

    Coach Name: _____ E-mail: _____

    Coach Telephone Number: _____

48. College Name: _____ Web Site: _____

    NCAA ___ DI ___ DII ___ DIII   ___ NAIA   ___JC

    Coach Name: _____ E-mail: _____

    Coach Telephone Number: _____

49. College Name: _____ Web Site: _____

    NCAA ___ DI ___ DII ___ DIII   ___ NAIA   ___JC

    Coach Name: _____ E-mail: _____

    Coach Telephone Number: _____

50. College Name: _____ Web Site: _____

   NCAA ___ DI ___ DII ___ DIII   ___ NAIA   ___JC

   Coach Name: _____ E-mail: _____

   Coach Telephone Number: _____

51. College Name: _____ Web Site: _____

   NCAA ___ DI ___ DII ___ DIII   ___ NAIA   ___JC

   Coach Name: _____ E-mail: _____

   Coach Telephone Number: _____

52. College Name: _____ Web Site: _____

   NCAA ___ DI ___ DII ___ DIII   ___ NAIA   ___JC

   Coach Name: _____ E-mail: _____

   Coach Telephone Number: _____

53. College Name: _____ Web Site: _____

   NCAA ___ DI ___ DII ___ DIII   ___ NAIA   ___JC

   Coach Name: _____ E-mail: _____

   Coach Telephone Number: _____

54. College Name: _____ Web Site: _____

   NCAA ___ DI ___ DII ___ DIII   ___ NAIA   ___JC

   Coach Name: _____ E-mail: _____

   Coach Telephone Number: _____

55. College Name: _____ Web Site: _____

    NCAA ___ DI ___ DII ___ DIII   ___ NAIA   ___JC

    Coach Name: _____ E-mail: _____

    Coach Telephone Number: _____

56. College Name: _____ Web Site: _____

    NCAA ___ DI ___ DII ___ DIII   ___ NAIA   ___JC

    Coach Name: _____ E-mail: _____

    Coach Telephone Number: _____

57. College Name: _____ Web Site: _____

    NCAA ___ DI ___ DII ___ DIII   ___ NAIA   ___JC

    Coach Name: _____ E-mail: _____

    Coach Telephone Number: _____

58. College Name: _____ Web Site: _____

    NCAA ___ DI ___ DII ___ DIII   ___ NAIA   ___JC

    Coach Name: _____ E-mail: _____

    Coach Telephone Number: _____

59. College Name: _____ Web Site: _____

    NCAA ___ DI ___ DII ___ DIII   ___ NAIA   ___JC

    Coach Name: _____ E-mail: _____

    Coach Telephone Number: _____

60. College Name: _____ Web Site: _____

    NCAA ___ DI ___ DII ___ DIII ___ NAIA ___JC

    Coach Name: _____ E-mail: _____

    Coach Telephone Number: _____

61. College Name: _____ Web Site: _____

    NCAA ___ DI ___ DII ___ DIII ___ NAIA ___JC

    Coach Name: _____ E-mail: _____

    Coach Telephone Number: _____

62. College Name: _____ Web Site: _____

    NCAA ___ DI ___ DII ___ DIII ___ NAIA ___JC

    Coach Name: _____ E-mail: _____

    Coach Telephone Number: _____

63. College Name: _____ Web Site: _____

    NCAA ___ DI ___ DII ___ DIII ___ NAIA ___JC

    Coach Name: _____ E-mail: _____

    Coach Telephone Number: _____

64. College Name: _____ Web Site: _____

    NCAA ___ DI ___ DII ___ DIII ___ NAIA ___JC

    Coach Name: _____ E-mail: _____

    Coach Telephone Number: _____

65. College Name: _____ Web Site: _____

    NCAA ___ DI ___ DII ___ DIII   ___ NAIA   ___JC

    Coach Name: _____ E-mail: _____

    Coach Telephone Number: _____

66. College Name: _____ Web Site: _____

    NCAA ___ DI ___ DII ___ DIII   ___ NAIA   ___JC

    Coach Name: _____ E-mail: _____

    Coach Telephone Number: _____

67. College Name: _____ Web Site: _____

    NCAA ___ DI ___ DII ___ DIII   ___ NAIA   ___JC

    Coach Name: _____ E-mail: _____

    Coach Telephone Number: _____

68. College Name: _____ Web Site: _____

    NCAA ___ DI ___ DII ___ DIII   ___ NAIA   ___JC

    Coach Name: _____ E-mail: _____

    Coach Telephone Number: _____

69. College Name: _____ Web Site: _____

    NCAA ___ DI ___ DII ___ DIII   ___ NAIA   ___JC

    Coach Name: _____ E-mail: _____

    Coach Telephone Number: _____

70. College Name: _____ Web Site: _____

    NCAA ___ DI ___ DII ___ DIII   ___ NAIA   ___JC

    Coach Name: _____ E-mail: _____

    Coach Telephone Number: _____

71. College Name: _____ Web Site: _____

    NCAA ___ DI ___ DII ___ DIII   ___ NAIA   ___JC

    Coach Name: _____ E-mail: _____

    Coach Telephone Number: _____

72. College Name: _____ Web Site: _____

    NCAA ___ DI ___ DII ___ DIII   ___ NAIA   ___JC

    Coach Name: _____ E-mail: _____

    Coach Telephone Number: _____

73. College Name: _____ Web Site: _____

    NCAA ___ DI ___ DII ___ DIII   ___ NAIA   ___JC

    Coach Name: _____ E-mail: _____

    Coach Telephone Number: _____

74. College Name: _____ Web Site: _____

    NCAA ___ DI ___ DII ___ DIII   ___ NAIA   ___JC

    Coach Name: _____ E-mail: _____

    Coach Telephone Number: _____

75. College Name: _____ Web Site: _____

    NCAA ___ DI ___ DII ___ DIII   ___ NAIA   ___JC

    Coach Name: _____ E-mail: _____

    Coach Telephone Number: _____

76. College Name: _____ Web Site: _____

    NCAA ___ DI ___ DII ___ DIII   ___ NAIA   ___JC

    Coach Name: _____ E-mail: _____

    Coach Telephone Number: _____

77. College Name: _____ Web Site: _____

    NCAA ___ DI ___ DII ___ DIII   ___ NAIA   ___JC

    Coach Name: _____ E-mail: _____

    Coach Telephone Number: _____

78. College Name: _____ Web Site: _____

    NCAA ___ DI ___ DII ___ DIII   ___ NAIA   ___JC

    Coach Name: _____ E-mail: _____

    Coach Telephone Number: _____

79. College Name: _____ Web Site: _____

    NCAA ___ DI ___ DII ___ DIII   ___ NAIA   ___JC

    Coach Name: _____ E-mail: _____

    Coach Telephone Number: _____

80. College Name: _____ Web Site: _____

    NCAA ___ DI ___ DII ___ DIII   ___ NAIA   ___JC

    Coach Name: _____ E-mail: _____

    Coach Telephone Number: _____

81. College Name: _____ Web Site: _____

    NCAA ___ DI ___ DII ___ DIII   ___ NAIA   ___JC

    Coach Name: _____ E-mail: _____

    Coach Telephone Number: _____

82. College Name: _____ Web Site: _____

    NCAA ___ DI ___ DII ___ DIII   ___ NAIA   ___JC

    Coach Name: _____ E-mail: _____

    Coach Telephone Number: _____

83. College Name: _____ Web Site: _____

    NCAA ___ DI ___ DII ___ DIII   ___ NAIA   ___JC

    Coach Name: _____ E-mail: _____

    Coach Telephone Number: _____

84. College Name: _____ Web Site: _____

    NCAA ___ DI ___ DII ___ DIII   ___ NAIA   ___JC

    Coach Name: _____ E-mail: _____

    Coach Telephone Number: _____

85. College Name: _____ Web Site: _____

    NCAA ___ DI ___ DII ___ DIII   ___ NAIA   ___JC

    Coach Name: _____ E-mail: _____

    Coach Telephone Number: _____

86. College Name: _____ Web Site: _____

    NCAA ___ DI ___ DII ___ DIII   ___ NAIA   ___JC

    Coach Name: _____ E-mail: _____

    Coach Telephone Number: _____

87. College Name: _____ Web Site: _____

    NCAA ___ DI ___ DII ___ DIII   ___ NAIA   ___JC

    Coach Name: _____ E-mail: _____

    Coach Telephone Number: _____

88. College Name: _____ Web Site: _____

    NCAA ___ DI ___ DII ___ DIII   ___ NAIA   ___JC

    Coach Name: _____ E-mail: _____

    Coach Telephone Number: _____

89. College Name: _____ Web Site: _____

    NCAA ___ DI ___ DII ___ DIII   ___ NAIA   ___JC

    Coach Name: _____ E-mail: _____

    Coach Telephone Number: _____

90. College Name: _____ Web Site: _____

    NCAA ___ DI ___ DII ___ DIII   ___ NAIA ___JC

    Coach Name: _____ E-mail: _____

    Coach Telephone Number: _____

91. College Name: _____ Web Site: _____

    NCAA ___ DI ___ DII ___ DIII   ___ NAIA ___JC

    Coach Name: _____ E-mail: _____

    Coach Telephone Number: _____

92. College Name: _____ Web Site: _____

    NCAA ___ DI ___ DII ___ DIII   ___ NAIA ___JC

    Coach Name: _____ E-mail: _____

    Coach Telephone Number: _____

93. College Name: _____ Web Site: _____

    NCAA ___ DI ___ DII ___ DIII   ___ NAIA ___JC

    Coach Name: _____ E-mail: _____

    Coach Telephone Number: _____

94. College Name: _____ Web Site: _____

    NCAA ___ DI ___ DII ___ DIII   ___ NAIA ___JC

    Coach Name: _____ E-mail: _____

    Coach Telephone Number: _____

95. College Name: _____ Web Site: _____

    NCAA ___ DI ___ DII ___ DIII   ___ NAIA   ___JC

    Coach Name: _____ E-mail: _____

    Coach Telephone Number: _____

96. College Name: _____ Web Site: _____

    NCAA ___ DI ___ DII ___ DIII   ___ NAIA   ___JC

    Coach Name: _____ E-mail: _____

    Coach Telephone Number: _____

97. College Name: _____ Web Site: _____

    NCAA ___ DI ___ DII ___ DIII   ___ NAIA   ___JC

    Coach Name: _____ E-mail: _____

    Coach Telephone Number: _____

98. College Name: _____ Web Site: _____

    NCAA ___ DI ___ DII ___ DIII   ___ NAIA   ___JC

    Coach Name: _____ E-mail: _____

    Coach Telephone Number: _____

99. College Name: _____ Web Site: _____

    NCAA ___ DI ___ DII ___ DIII   ___ NAIA   ___JC

    Coach Name: _____ E-mail: _____

    Coach Telephone Number: _____

100.   College Name: _____ Web Site: _____

NCAA ___ DI ___ DII ___ DIII   ___ NAIA   ___ JC

Coach Name: _____ E-mail: _____

Coach Telephone Number: _____

101.   College Name: _____ Web Site: _____

NCAA ___ DI ___ DII ___ DIII   ___ NAIA   ___ JC

Coach Name: _____ E-mail: _____

Coach Telephone Number: _____

102.   College Name: _____ Web Site: _____

NCAA ___ DI ___ DII ___ DIII   ___ NAIA   ___ JC

Coach Name: _____ E-mail: _____

Coach Telephone Number: _____

103.   College Name: _____ Web Site: _____

NCAA ___ DI ___ DII ___ DIII   ___ NAIA   ___ JC

Coach Name: _____ E-mail: _____

Coach Telephone Number: _____

104.   College Name: _____ Web Site: _____

NCAA ___ DI ___ DII ___ DIII   ___ NAIA   ___ JC

Coach Name: _____ E-mail: _____

Coach Telephone Number: _____

105. College Name: _____ Web Site: _____

NCAA ___ DI ___ DII ___ DIII   ___ NAIA   ___JC

Coach Name: _____ E-mail: _____

Coach Telephone Number: _____

106. College Name: _____ Web Site: _____

NCAA ___ DI ___ DII ___ DIII   ___ NAIA   ___JC

Coach Name: _____ E-mail: _____

Coach Telephone Number: _____

107. College Name: _____ Web Site: _____

NCAA ___ DI ___ DII ___ DIII   ___ NAIA   ___JC

Coach Name: _____ E-mail: _____

Coach Telephone Number: _____

108. College Name: _____ Web Site: _____

NCAA ___ DI ___ DII ___ DIII   ___ NAIA   ___JC

Coach Name: _____ E-mail: _____

Coach Telephone Number: _____

109. College Name: _____ Web Site: _____

NCAA ___ DI ___ DII ___ DIII   ___ NAIA   ___JC

Coach Name: _____ E-mail: _____

Coach Telephone Number: _____

110.   College Name: _____ Web Site: _____

NCAA ___ DI ___ DII ___ DIII   ___ NAIA   ___JC

Coach Name: _____ E-mail: _____

Coach Telephone Number: _____

111.   College Name: _____ Web Site: _____

NCAA ___ DI ___ DII ___ DIII   ___ NAIA   ___JC

Coach Name: _____ E-mail: _____

Coach Telephone Number: _____

112.   College Name: _____ Web Site: _____

NCAA ___ DI ___ DII ___ DIII   ___ NAIA   ___JC

Coach Name: _____ E-mail: _____

Coach Telephone Number: _____

113.   College Name: _____ Web Site: _____

NCAA ___ DI ___ DII ___ DIII   ___ NAIA   ___JC

Coach Name: _____ E-mail: _____

Coach Telephone Number: _____

114.   College Name: _____ Web Site: _____

NCAA ___ DI ___ DII ___ DIII   ___ NAIA   ___JC

Coach Name: _____ E-mail: _____

Coach Telephone Number: _____

115.   College Name: _____ Web Site: _____

NCAA ___ DI ___ DII ___ DIII   ___ NAIA   ___JC

Coach Name: _____ E-mail: _____

Coach Telephone Number: _____

116.   College Name: _____ Web Site: _____

NCAA ___ DI ___ DII ___ DIII   ___ NAIA   ___JC

Coach Name: _____ E-mail: _____

Coach Telephone Number: _____

117.   College Name: _____ Web Site: _____

NCAA ___ DI ___ DII ___ DIII   ___ NAIA   ___JC

Coach Name: _____ E-mail: _____

Coach Telephone Number: _____

118.   College Name: _____ Web Site: _____

NCAA ___ DI ___ DII ___ DIII   ___ NAIA   ___JC

Coach Name: _____ E-mail: _____

Coach Telephone Number: _____

119.   College Name: _____ Web Site: _____

NCAA ___ DI ___ DII ___ DIII   ___ NAIA   ___JC

Coach Name: _____ E-mail: _____

Coach Telephone Number: _____

120.   College Name: _____ Web Site: _____

NCAA ___ DI ___ DII ___ DIII   ___ NAIA   ___JC

Coach Name: _____ E-mail: _____

Coach Telephone Number: _____

121.   College Name: _____ Web Site: _____

NCAA ___ DI ___ DII ___ DIII   ___ NAIA   ___JC

Coach Name: _____ E-mail: _____

Coach Telephone Number: _____

122.   College Name: _____ Web Site: _____

NCAA ___ DI ___ DII ___ DIII   ___ NAIA   ___JC

Coach Name: _____ E-mail: _____

Coach Telephone Number: _____

123.   College Name: _____ Web Site: _____

NCAA ___ DI ___ DII ___ DIII   ___ NAIA   ___JC

Coach Name: _____ E-mail: _____

Coach Telephone Number: _____

124.   College Name: _____ Web Site: _____

NCAA ___ DI ___ DII ___ DIII   ___ NAIA   ___JC

Coach Name: _____ E-mail: _____

Coach Telephone Number: _____

125.   College Name: _____ Web Site: _____

    NCAA ___ DI ___ DII ___ DIII   ___ NAIA ___ JC

    Coach Name: _____ E-mail: _____

    Coach Telephone Number: _____

126.   College Name: _____ Web Site: _____

    NCAA ___ DI ___ DII ___ DIII   ___ NAIA ___ JC

    Coach Name: _____ E-mail: _____

    Coach Telephone Number: _____

127.   College Name: _____ Web Site: _____

    NCAA ___ DI ___ DII ___ DIII   ___ NAIA ___ JC

    Coach Name: _____ E-mail: _____

    Coach Telephone Number: _____

128.   College Name: _____ Web Site: _____

    NCAA ___ DI ___ DII ___ DIII   ___ NAIA ___ JC

    Coach Name: _____ E-mail: _____

    Coach Telephone Number: _____

129.   College Name: _____ Web Site: _____

    NCAA ___ DI ___ DII ___ DIII   ___ NAIA ___ JC

    Coach Name: _____ E-mail: _____

    Coach Telephone Number: _____

130.	College Name: _____ Web Site: _____

NCAA ___ DI ___ DII ___ DIII   ___ NAIA   ___JC

Coach Name: _____ E-mail: _____

Coach Telephone Number: _____

131.	College Name: _____ Web Site: _____

NCAA ___ DI ___ DII ___ DIII   ___ NAIA   ___JC

Coach Name: _____ E-mail: _____

Coach Telephone Number: _____

132.	College Name: _____ Web Site: _____

NCAA ___ DI ___ DII ___ DIII   ___ NAIA   ___JC

Coach Name: _____ E-mail: _____

Coach Telephone Number: _____

133.	College Name: _____ Web Site: _____

NCAA ___ DI ___ DII ___ DIII   ___ NAIA   ___JC

Coach Name: _____ E-mail: _____

Coach Telephone Number: _____

134.	College Name: _____ Web Site: _____

NCAA ___ DI ___ DII ___ DIII   ___ NAIA   ___JC

Coach Name: _____ E-mail: _____

Coach Telephone Number: _____

135.　College Name: _____ Web Site: _____

NCAA ___ DI ___ DII ___ DIII   ___ NAIA   ___JC

Coach Name: _____ E-mail: _____

Coach Telephone Number: _____

136.　College Name: _____ Web Site: _____

NCAA ___ DI ___ DII ___ DIII   ___ NAIA   ___JC

Coach Name: _____ E-mail: _____

Coach Telephone Number: _____

137.　College Name: _____ Web Site: _____

NCAA ___ DI ___ DII ___ DIII   ___ NAIA   ___JC

Coach Name: _____ E-mail: _____

Coach Telephone Number: _____

138.　College Name: _____ Web Site: _____

NCAA ___ DI ___ DII ___ DIII   ___ NAIA   ___JC

Coach Name: _____ E-mail: _____

Coach Telephone Number: _____

139.　College Name: _____ Web Site: _____

NCAA ___ DI ___ DII ___ DIII   ___ NAIA   ___JC

Coach Name: _____ E-mail: _____

Coach Telephone Number: _____

140.   College Name: _____ Web Site: _____

NCAA ___ DI ___ DII ___ DIII   ___ NAIA   ___JC

Coach Name: _____ E-mail: _____

Coach Telephone Number: _____

141.   College Name: _____ Web Site: _____

NCAA ___ DI ___ DII ___ DIII   ___ NAIA   ___JC

Coach Name: _____ E-mail: _____

Coach Telephone Number: _____

142.   College Name: _____ Web Site: _____

NCAA ___ DI ___ DII ___ DIII   ___ NAIA   ___JC

Coach Name: _____ E-mail: _____

Coach Telephone Number: _____

143.   College Name: _____ Web Site: _____

NCAA ___ DI ___ DII ___ DIII   ___ NAIA   ___JC

Coach Name: _____ E-mail: _____

Coach Telephone Number: _____

144.   College Name: _____ Web Site: _____

NCAA ___ DI ___ DII ___ DIII   ___ NAIA   ___JC

Coach Name: _____ E-mail: _____

Coach Telephone Number: _____

145.   College Name: _____ Web Site: _____

NCAA ___ DI ___ DII ___ DIII   ___ NAIA   ___JC

Coach Name: _____ E-mail: _____

Coach Telephone Number: _____

146.   College Name: _____ Web Site: _____

NCAA ___ DI ___ DII ___ DIII   ___ NAIA   ___JC

Coach Name: _____ E-mail: _____

Coach Telephone Number: _____

147.   College Name: _____ Web Site: _____

NCAA ___ DI ___ DII ___ DIII   ___ NAIA   ___JC

Coach Name: _____ E-mail: _____

Coach Telephone Number: _____

148.   College Name: _____ Web Site: _____

NCAA ___ DI ___ DII ___ DIII   ___ NAIA   ___JC

Coach Name: _____ E-mail: _____

Coach Telephone Number: _____

149.   College Name: _____ Web Site: _____

NCAA ___ DI ___ DII ___ DIII   ___ NAIA   ___JC

Coach Name: _____ E-mail: _____

Coach Telephone Number: _____

Safety Schools: **Date:** _____

1. College Name: _____ Web Site: _____

    NCAA ___ DI ___ DII ___ DIII   ___ NAIA   ___JC

    Coach Name: _____ E-mail: _____

    Coach Telephone Number: _____

2. College Name: _____ Web Site: _____

    NCAA ___ DI ___ DII ___ DIII   ___ NAIA   ___JC

    Coach Name: _____ E-mail: _____

    Coach Telephone Number: _____

3. College Name: _____ Web Site: _____

    NCAA ___ DI ___ DII ___ DIII   ___ NAIA   ___JC

    Coach Name: _____ E-mail: _____

    Coach Telephone Number: _____

4. College Name: _____ Web Site: _____

    NCAA ___ DI ___ DII ___ DIII   ___ NAIA   ___JC

    Coach Name: _____ E-mail: _____

    Coach Telephone Number: _____

5. College Name: _____ Web Site: _____

 NCAA ___ DI ___ DII ___ DIII ___ NAIA ___JC

 Coach Name: _____ E-mail: _____

 Coach Telephone Number: _____

6. College Name: _____ Web Site: _____

 NCAA ___ DI ___ DII ___ DIII ___ NAIA ___JC

 Coach Name: _____ E-mail: _____

 Coach Telephone Number: _____

7. College Name: _____ Web Site: _____

 NCAA ___ DI ___ DII ___ DIII ___ NAIA ___JC

 Coach Name: _____ E-mail: _____

 Coach Telephone Number: _____

8. College Name: _____ Web Site: _____

 NCAA ___ DI ___ DII ___ DIII ___ NAIA ___JC

 Coach Name: _____ E-mail: _____

 Coach Telephone Number: _____

9. College Name: _____ Web Site: _____

 NCAA ___ DI ___ DII ___ DIII ___ NAIA ___JC

 Coach Name: _____ E-mail: _____

 Coach Telephone Number: _____

10. College Name: _____ Web Site: _____

    NCAA ___ DI ___ DII ___ DIII   ___ NAIA   ___ JC

    Coach Name: _____ E-mail: _____

    Coach Telephone Number: _____

11. College Name: _____ Web Site: _____

    NCAA ___ DI ___ DII ___ DIII   ___ NAIA   ___ JC

    Coach Name: _____ E-mail: _____

    Coach Telephone Number: _____

12. College Name: _____ Web Site: _____

    NCAA ___ DI ___ DII ___ DIII   ___ NAIA   ___ JC

    Coach Name: _____ E-mail: _____

    Coach Telephone Number: _____

13. College Name: _____ Web Site: _____

    NCAA ___ DI ___ DII ___ DIII   ___ NAIA   ___ JC

    Coach Name: _____ E-mail: _____

    Coach Telephone Number: _____

14. College Name: _____ Web Site: _____

    NCAA ___ DI ___ DII ___ DIII   ___ NAIA   ___ JC

    Coach Name: _____ E-mail: _____

    Coach Telephone Number: _____

Other/Maybe: **Date:** _____

1. College Name: _____ Web Site: _____

    NCAA ___ DI ___ DII ___ DIII   ___ NAIA   ___JC

    Coach Name: _____ E-mail: _____

    Coach Telephone Number: _____

2. College Name: _____ Web Site: _____

    NCAA ___ DI ___ DII ___ DIII   ___ NAIA   ___JC

    Coach Name: _____ E-mail: _____

    Coach Telephone Number: _____

3. College Name: _____ Web Site: _____

    NCAA ___ DI ___ DII ___ DIII   ___ NAIA   ___JC

    Coach Name: _____ E-mail: _____

    Coach Telephone Number: _____

4. College Name: _____ Web Site: _____

    NCAA ___ DI ___ DII ___ DIII   ___ NAIA   ___JC

    Coach Name: _____ E-mail: _____

    Coach Telephone Number: _____

5. College Name: _____ Web Site: _____

   NCAA ___ DI ___ DII ___ DIII   ___ NAIA   ___JC

   Coach Name: _____ E-mail: _____

   Coach Telephone Number: _____

6. College Name: _____ Web Site: _____

   NCAA ___ DI ___ DII ___ DIII   ___ NAIA   ___JC

   Coach Name: _____ E-mail: _____

   Coach Telephone Number: _____

7. College Name: _____ Web Site: _____

   NCAA ___ DI ___ DII ___ DIII   ___ NAIA   ___JC

   Coach Name: _____ E-mail: _____

   Coach Telephone Number: _____

8. College Name: _____ Web Site: _____

   NCAA ___ DI ___ DII ___ DIII   ___ NAIA   ___JC

   Coach Name: _____ E-mail: _____

   Coach Telephone Number: _____

9. College Name: _____ Web Site: _____

   NCAA ___ DI ___ DII ___ DIII   ___ NAIA   ___JC

   Coach Name: _____ E-mail: _____

   Coach Telephone Number: _____

10. College Name: _____ Web Site: _____

    NCAA ___ DI ___ DII ___ DIII   ___ NAIA   ___JC

    Coach Name: _____ E-mail: _____

    Coach Telephone Number: _____

11. College Name: _____ Web Site: _____

    NCAA ___ DI ___ DII ___ DIII   ___ NAIA   ___JC

    Coach Name: _____ E-mail: _____

    Coach Telephone Number: _____

12. College Name: _____ Web Site: _____

    NCAA ___ DI ___ DII ___ DIII   ___ NAIA   ___JC

    Coach Name: _____ E-mail: _____

    Coach Telephone Number: _____

13. College Name: _____ Web Site: _____

    NCAA ___ DI ___ DII ___ DIII   ___ NAIA   ___JC

    Coach Name: _____ E-mail: _____

    Coach Telephone Number: _____

14. College Name: _____ Web Site: _____

    NCAA ___ DI ___ DII ___ DIII   ___ NAIA   ___JC

    Coach Name: _____ E-mail: _____

    Coach Telephone Number: _____

Coach Contacted Me But Not On My List: Date: _____

1. College Name: _____ Web Site: _____

    NCAA ___ DI ___ DII ___ DIII   ___ NAIA   ___JC

    Coach Name: _____ E-mail: _____

    Coach Telephone Number: _____

2. College Name: _____ Web Site: _____

    NCAA ___ DI ___ DII ___ DIII   ___ NAIA   ___JC

    Coach Name: _____ E-mail: _____

    Coach Telephone Number: _____

3. College Name: _____ Web Site: _____

    NCAA ___ DI ___ DII ___ DIII   ___ NAIA   ___JC

    Coach Name: _____ E-mail: _____

    Coach Telephone Number: _____

4. College Name: _____ Web Site: _____

    NCAA ___ DI ___ DII ___ DIII   ___ NAIA   ___JC

    Coach Name: _____ E-mail: _____

    Coach Telephone Number: _____

5. College Name: _____ Web Site: _____

    NCAA ___ DI ___ DII ___ DIII   ___ NAIA   ___JC

    Coach Name: _____ E-mail: _____

    Coach Telephone Number: _____

6. College Name: _____ Web Site: _____

    NCAA ___ DI ___ DII ___ DIII   ___ NAIA   ___JC

    Coach Name: _____ E-mail: _____

    Coach Telephone Number: _____

7. College Name: _____ Web Site: _____

    NCAA ___ DI ___ DII ___ DIII   ___ NAIA   ___JC

    Coach Name: _____ E-mail: _____

    Coach Telephone Number: _____

8. College Name: _____ Web Site: _____

    NCAA ___ DI ___ DII ___ DIII   ___ NAIA   ___JC

    Coach Name: _____ E-mail: _____

    Coach Telephone Number: _____

9. College Name: _____ Web Site: _____

    NCAA ___ DI ___ DII ___ DIII   ___ NAIA   ___JC

    Coach Name: _____ E-mail: _____

    Coach Telephone Number: _____

10. College Name: _____ Web Site: _____

    NCAA ___ DI ___ DII ___ DIII   ___ NAIA   ___JC

    Coach Name: _____ E-mail: _____

    Coach Telephone Number: _____

11. College Name: _____ Web Site: _____

    NCAA ___ DI ___ DII ___ DIII   ___ NAIA   ___JC

    Coach Name: _____ E-mail: _____

    Coach Telephone Number: _____

12. College Name: _____ Web Site: _____

    NCAA ___ DI ___ DII ___ DIII   ___ NAIA   ___JC

    Coach Name: _____ E-mail: _____

    Coach Telephone Number: _____

13. College Name: _____ Web Site: _____

    NCAA ___ DI ___ DII ___ DIII   ___ NAIA   ___JC

    Coach Name: _____ E-mail: _____

    Coach Telephone Number: _____

14. College Name: _____ Web Site: _____

    NCAA ___ DI ___ DII ___ DIII   ___ NAIA   ___JC

    Coach Name: _____ E-mail: _____

    Coach Telephone Number: _____

CPSIA information can be obtained at www.ICGtesting.com
262620BV00003B/1/P